More Crocheted Aran Sweaters

Jane Snedden Peever

Martingale®
& COMPANY

More Crocheted Aran Sweaters

© 2005 by Jane Snedden Peever

Martingale & Company

20205 144th Avenue NE

Woodinville, WA 98072-8478 USA

www.martingale-pub.com

For showing me the world through the creative, enthusiastic eyes of a child, this book is for my two little angels, Tessa and Thomas.

MISSION STATEMENT
Dedicated to providing quality products and service to inspire creativity.

Credits

President: Nancy J. Martin
CEO: Daniel J. Martin
VP and General Manager: Tom Wierzbicki
Publisher: Jane Hamada
Editorial Director: Mary V. Green
Managing Editor: Tina Cook
Technical Editor: Ursula Reikes
Copy Editor: Ellen Balstad
Design Director and Cover Designer: Stan Green
Stitch Illustrator: Laurel Strand

Produced by

Huxley Communications LLC,
Easton, Pennsylvania

Managing Editor, Acquisitions, and
  Technical Editor: Susan Huxley
Design and Layout Artist: Barbara Field
Schematics Illustrator: Barbara Field
Cover and Fashion Photographer: J. P. Hamel
Stitch Detail Photographer: Robert Gerheart
Hair and Makeup Artist: Colleen Kubrick-Kuehne
  Fashion photography was shot in the historic district of Easton, Pennsylvania, and at the home of the Foster family in East Greenville, Pennsylvania.

Printed in China
10 09 08 07 06 05   8 7 6 5 4 3 2 1

Library of Congress Cataloging-in-Publication Data
Peever, Jane Snedden.
  More crocheted Aran sweaters/Jane Snedden
  Peever.
    p. cm.
  ISBN 1-56477-590-9
  1. Crocheting–Ireland–Aran Islands–Patterns. 2.
  Sweaters–Ireland–Aran Islands. I. Title.
  TT819.I74A727 2005
  746.43'40432–dc22
                                2005003485

Contents

Glorious Cables

Celebrate crochet with old-world patternwork and a medley of stitches.

Is there anything more wonderful than a crocheted fabric that's covered with stitches twining and weaving across the surface? Textured effects and ever-present cables attest to the skill and patience of a talented stitcher while silently acknowledging a rich Irish heritage.

For generations, people around the world have admired this distinct patternwork that originated in the Aran Islands. Aran patternwork is commonly thought to be the preserve of knitters, but designer Jane Snedden Peever proves that it is within the grasp of any crocheter. Now you, too, can enjoy watching motifs grow as you work raised posts on a bed of single crochet stitches.

In this, her second book, Jane again brings her modern sensibility to this traditional work. Borrowing well-loved motifs as well as developing her own distinct interpretations, Jane has created 12 classic sweaters, a vest, and even more new stitch patterns for you to crochet.

The beauty of her Aran patternwork is that the finished garments look more complex than they really are. As with her first book, *Crocheted Aran Sweaters*, Jane continues to work primarily with basic stitches: the chain, slip, single, half double, double, and treble. A crocheter who can make these stitches already has the knowledge and skill to master the dozen stitch variations that are used to make all of the garments in this book. Regardless of your skills, in *More Crocheted Aran Sweaters* you'll find a stitch pattern and sweater or vest that matches your skills. And, because the instructions are presented in a wide range of sizes and many have unisex styling, you're sure to find a sweater that suits your wardrobe. To begin your adventure, start by reading the advice and tips in the "Patternwork Primer" starting on the next page, choose your sweater, and then review the stitches you need to learn by looking them up in the "Featured Stitches Guide" on page 84.

The pride you'll feel upon completing your garment will only be matched by the compliments and admiration you'll receive when you wear it or the joy you'll share when you give it as a gift. The lush texture and stitches of Aran patternwork are yours for the making.

Susan Huxley

Patternwork Primer

The beauty of an Aran sweater is, perhaps, the mystique of its intricate patterning. Yet truth be told, the Aran sweaters in this book are designed to be less challenging than they look. Some garments, such as Country Lane (page 21), Double Spiral (page 47), and Double Feature (page 59), can be made by a beginning crocheter. Others, however, are best tackled by a stitcher with some experience. Whatever your skill level, this chapter offers tips and techniques that will ease the creative process.

Picking Your Size

Once you've fallen in love with the sweater or vest that you want to make, check out the finished garment measurements. Here's the great news: the instructions are for an exceptionally large range of sizes. Two of the sweaters are sized to fit a 48" bust or chest. The rest of the patterns are offered in five sizes, from Extra Small (31" bust) to Extra Large (43¼" bust). Don't automatically assume that you're the size you usually wear. Check the bust/chest measurements.

Swatching Stitch Patterns

You've probably encountered instructions where you've had to dig around for the core stitches and rows that make up the pattern. *More Crocheted Aran Sweaters* has eased this process for you by placing the swatch instructions at the beginning of every sweater project. This section offers additional guidance that you won't find in the garment piece instructions.

Underneath the stitch pattern name is a very important tidbit that's easy to overlook. Almost all stitch patterns consist of repeats, or multiples. A certain group of stitches (usually the ones placed between asterisks [*] in the body of instructions) are made again and again across a row. When you work a swatch, you need to have enough stitches to make several full repeats. For example, the Repeating Cables stitch pattern in Emerald Isle (page 33) has a 6-stitch multiple. You might want to work three repeats in a swatch, so you need 18 stitches. You need to add additional stitches that set up the beginning and end of each row. For the Repeating Cables stitch pattern, it's "+ 3." Now the swatch is up to 21 stitches.

Of course, since a chain stitch is "lost" when you make the first row of single crochet stitches, the final bit of information for your swatch is a simple reminder to add that extra stitch to the base chain. So, to work the Repeating Cables stitch pattern, you'd chain 22 stitches, and then follow the row-by-row instructions. Make sure that you work enough stitches and rows to make a swatch for checking your gauge!

▓ *Learning Stitches*

Testing the stitch pattern goes hand in hand with learning the stitches. Many of the cables, textures, and twisted stitches in *More Crocheted Aran Sweaters* were invented just for this book. As you work up a test swatch, you'll need to look up a stitch or two in the "Featured Stitches Guide." Don't let this extra step discourage you. If you've been stitching for years, ask yourself when you last experienced the thrill of learning a new stitch. If you're new to crocheting, keep in mind that cables and crossed stitches are built on basics.

Aran patternwork is all about post stitches. These are little more than double or treble crochets that are worked in the row below, around the center—rather than the top or base—of a stitch. Start by mastering the front post double crochet on page 88. Then move on to the stitches that are required for the sweater that you want to make. Try not to work too tightly as this makes it difficult to work into stitches in the previous row. It's easier to insert your hook in the right spot if you and your work are relaxed.

Don't get frustrated if it takes time to develop your new skills. Aran sweaters are classic and well worth the time and effort that you'll put into each one.

▓ *Checking Gauge*

The instructions for every sweater pattern include the number of stitches and rows that you need in a 4" square. In a few cases, the gauge is specified over fewer inches because a panel is narrower.

If two stitch patterns are prominent in the sweater, it's best to check the gauge for both. Depending on your stitching technique, you may have to switch to a larger or smaller hook while working one of the stitch patterns. Again, this book makes this process easier for you. Where you need to test more than one stitch pattern, the sweater instructions will list the gauge and row-by-row instructions for both.

If your stitch and row counts don't match the sweater gauge, don't start the garment pieces yet. Only half a stitch extra can have disastrous consequences to the fit of the finished sweater. Switch to a larger hook if you need fewer stitches or rows—or a smaller hook for more stitches or rows—and make another swatch.

▓ *Establishing Edge Stitches*

Almost all of the sweaters in this book are designed with one single crochet stitch at the beginning and end of every row. These edge stitches can be part of the stitch pattern repeat or they may be extra stitches.

When necessary, instructions introduce additional edge stitches when the shaping or stitch pattern setup begins. Even if you choose to work partial stitch pattern repeats while shaping (see "Working Partial Stitch Repeats" on the next page), maintain the single crochet edge stitches. They'll help you identify the beginning and end of your repeats, and they'll create a nice border for seaming.

▓ *Changing Colors*

Several of the sweaters feature color work, yet you don't need to carry strands across the back of the crocheted fabric. Every row is worked in a single color. If you need to start a new color in the next row, merely change the color in the last stitch of the row. This technique is optional, but it does yield a neater edge.

1 Work across the row in the current color (yarn A). At the end of the row, insert the hook into the last stitch, wrap yarn A around the hook, draw through a loop, and drop A.

2 Leaving a 3" tail, wrap yarn B around the hook, draw the yarn B loop through both yarn A loops on the hook.

3 Cut yarn A, leaving a 3" tail to sew in later. Turn the work and proceed as directed with yarn B for the next row.

Note: In the rare instance where the last stitch is not a single crochet, just work the last yarn over with yarn B.

▓ *Shaping Garment Pieces*

The sweaters in this book are designed with a minimum of shaping. You may find that the garment you love has straight sides and only a few skipped stitches at the front neckline. Sleeves, which must be shaped to some degree so that they look attractive, are often designed with simple stitch patterns so that the increases at the edges aren't too problematic.

When increasing or decreasing encroaches on a pattern repeat, you have two options: work only full pattern repeats or make partial pattern repeats on the shaping row. The easiest way to deal with shaping is to work only full repeats of the stitch pattern across a decrease or increase row. The processes are explained here.

Decreasing with Complete Stitch Repeats

1 In the last row without shaping, place a marker before the first stitch of the first pattern repeat. At the end of the row, place another marker after the last stitch of the last repeat. There may be one or more single crochet stitches outside the markers.

2 Make the decrease at the beginning of the row. If you only had one single crochet edge stitch, the marker is in the second stitch in the previous row. The decrease you just made used the stitch with the marker in it. Remove the marker. Find the beginning of the next stitch pattern repeat in the previous row. (This is to the last stitch of the second-to-the-last repeat you made when working the previous row.) Place the marker in that stitch.

3 Work the stitch pattern as established across the row. Stop when you're near the end. Count the remaining stitches to the marker. If there are too few to make another repeat, move the marker to the end of the last full repeat worked in the current row.

4 Switch to single crochet stitches and work to the end or the location of the next decrease.

Increasing with Complete Stitch Repeats

1 In the last row without shaping, place a marker before the first stitch of the first pattern repeat. At the end of the row, place another marker after the last stitch of the last repeat. There may be one or more single crochet stitches outside the markers. If the stitch pattern is worked from the first to the last stitch of a row, follow the steps in "Tracking Stitch Patterns" before starting step 2.

2 Increase at the beginning and end of the row as specified, working the stitch pattern between the markers.

3 When you have added enough stitches at each edge to work an entire repeat plus an edge stitch, move the markers outward. Climbing Cables (see page 16), for example, has an eight-stitch repeat. When the start of a row has nine stitches before the marker, and another nine stitches after the second marker, shift the markers so that one is between the first and second stitch, and the other is between the second-to-the-last stitch and the last stitch.

4 On the next row, work the established pattern between the markers, with a single crochet stitch at each edge.

Tracking Stitch Patterns

In some sweaters, there are sizes that have repeats from the very first to the last stitch in a row. In other words, there are no edge stitches for those sizes. These require a different approach to increases. The step-by-step directions follow.

1 Work an increase in the first stitch of the row, and then make the first stitch of the repeat. Here's an example: "Ch 1 (do not count as st), sc in first st (inc made), hdc in first st (patt rep started)..."

2 Place a stitch marker between the first (new) stitch and the next stitch. At the end of the row, work the last stitch of the final pattern repeat, and then make the increase in the last stitch. Place another marker between the last two stitches you just worked.

3 In the next row, work the stitch pattern between the markers and single crochet into the edge stitches, which are outside the markers.

4 Maintaining the stitch pattern between the markers as established, you can continue increasing stitches at the edges. Work the new stitches as single crochet.

Working Partial Stitch Repeats

By the time you've worked enough of a garment piece to start shaping the edges, you've worked the stitch pattern so often that you probably have a lot of confidence. In this case, you might want to start or end a row with only part of a stitch pattern worked. Partial repeats continue the pattern into even small areas. In Garden Gate, for example, the top of the raglan sleeve shown in the photo on page 55 is worked with the end of one repeat and the start of the next.

For this approach, think like a chess player and plan ahead. If, for example, you make two front post double crochet stitches near the start of the current row, ask yourself if the decrease on the next right-side row will interfere with the completion of the two-stitch cable (cb2, page 85) or post stitch cross (cr2, page 87) that you just started.

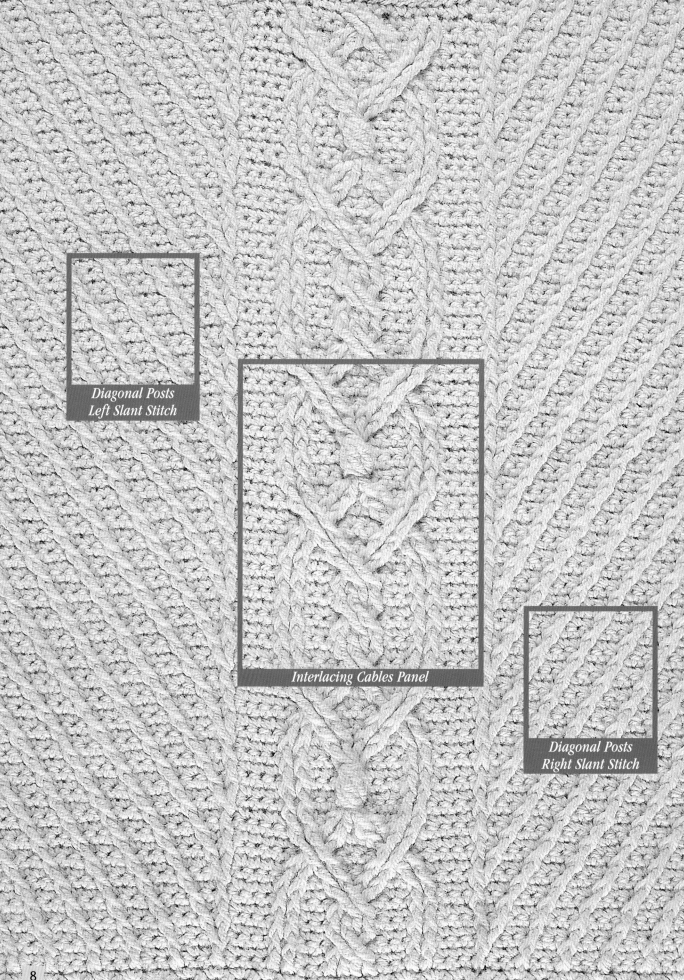

Diagonal Posts
Left Slant Stitch

Interlacing Cables Panel

Diagonal Posts
Right Slant Stitch

A graceful central panel and bold diagonals lend casual elegance to this pullover. Bulk-free yet warm, the garment features straight sides, drop shoulders, and a basic crew neck. The garment front and back showcase an intricate pattern that uses advanced stitches. It also has a combination of increase and decrease posts that create a unique bobble.

YARN
Snow Goose from Skacel, color #3005 Aran

Extra Small	•	12 balls
Small	•	12 balls
Medium	•	13 balls
Large	•	14 balls
Extra Large	•	15 balls

SUPPLIES
7 (4.5 mm) crochet hook
H/8 (5 mm) crochet hook
4 stitch markers

GAUGE
14 sts and 16 rows to 4" in Interlacing Cables st patt with H/8 (5 mm) hook
14 sts and 16 rows to 4" in Diagonal Posts Right Slant st patt with H/8 (5 mm) hook

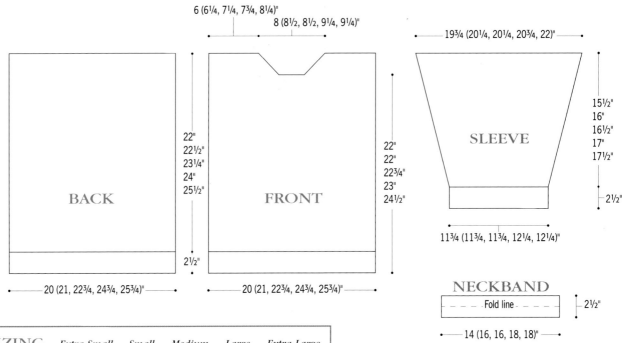

6 (6¼, 7¼, 7¾, 8¼)"

8 (8½, 8½, 9¼, 9¼)"

19¾ (20¼, 20¼, 20¾, 22)"

BACK

22"
22½"
23¼"
24"
25½"

2½"

FRONT

22"
22"
22¾"
23"
24½"

SLEEVE

15½"
16"
16½"
17"
17½"

2½"

11¾ (11¾, 11¾, 12¼, 12¼)"

20 (21, 22¾, 24¾, 25¾)"

20 (21, 22¾, 24¾, 25¾)"

NECKBAND

- - - - Fold line - - - -

2½"

14 (16, 16, 18, 18)"

SIZING	Extra Small	Small	Medium	Large	Extra Large
To fit bust	31½"	34¼"	37¼"	41"	43¼"
Finished bust	40"	42"	45½"	49½"	51½"
Shoulder width	6"	6¼"	7¼"	7¾"	8¼"
Sleeve length	18"	18½"	19"	19½"	20"
Center back length	24½"	25"	25¾"	26½"	28"

DIAGONAL POSTS RIGHT SLANT STITCH PATTERN

Multiple of 3 sts + 6 sts (also add 1 ch for base ch)

FOUNDATION ROW (RS): Sc in 2nd ch from hk (count as st) and in each ch to end, turn.

Row 2: Ch 1, sc in first and each st to end, turn.

Row 3: Ch 1, sc in first st, FPDC around next sc in row below (second st from edge or st marker), *sc in each of next 2 sts, FPDC around next sc in row below (third st from last FPDC)*, rep from * to * to last st, sc in last st, turn.

Rows 4, 6, and 8: Ch 1, sc in first st and each st to end, turn.

Row 5: Ch 1, sc in each of first 3 sts, *TWR, sc in next st*, rep from * to * to last 3 sts, 2 FPDC around next FPDC, sc in last st, turn.

Row 7: Ch 1, sc in each of first 2 sts, *TWR, sc in next st*, rep from * to * to last 4 sts, TWR, FPDC around next FPDC, sc in last st, turn.

Row 9: Ch 1, sc in first st, *TWR, sc in next st*, rep from * to * to last 2 sts, FPDC around next FPDC, sc in last st, turn.

Rows 4–9 form Diagonal Posts Right Slant st patt rep.

DIAGONAL POSTS LEFT SLANT STITCH PATTERN

Multiple of 3 sts + 6 sts (also add 1 ch for base ch)

FOUNDATION ROW (RS): Sc in 2nd ch from hk (count as st) and in each ch to end, turn.

Row 2: Ch 1, sc in first and each st to end, turn.

Row 3: Ch 1, sc in first st, FPDC around next sc in row below (second st from edge or st marker), *sc in each of next 2 sts, FPDC around next sc in row below (third st from last FPDC)*, rep from * to * to last st, sc in last st, turn.

Rows 4, 6, and 8: Ch 1, sc in first st and each st to end, turn.

Row 5: Ch 1, sc in first st, 2 FPDC around first FPDC, sc in next st, *TWL, sc in next st*, rep from * to * to last 2 sts, sc in each of last 2 sts, turn.

Row 7: Ch 1, sc in first st, FPDC around first FPDC, TWL over next (second) FPDC and next sc, sc in next st, *TWL, sc in next st*, rep from * to * to last st, sc in last st, turn.

Row 9: Ch 1, sc in first st, FPDC around first FPDC, sc in next st, *TWL, sc in next st*, rep from * to * to end, turn.

Rows 4–9 form Diagonal Posts Left Slant st patt rep.

▌INTERLACING CABLES PANEL

16 sts (also add 1 ch for base ch)

Foundation Row (RS): Sc in 2nd ch from hk (count as st) and in each ch to end, turn.

Row 2: Ch 1, sc in first and each st to end, turn.

Row 3: Ch 1, sc in each of first 2 sts, FPDC around each of next 2 sc in row below (third and fourth sts from edge or marker), sc in each of next 2 sts, FPDC around each of next 4 sc in row below (third, fourth, fifth and sixth sts from last FPDC), sc in each of next 2 sts, FPDC around each of next 2 sc in row below (third and fourth sts from last FPDC), sc in each of last 2 sts, turn.

Row 4 and Every WS Row: Ch 1, sc in first and each st to end, turn.

Row 5: Ch 1, sc in each of first 2 sts, FPDC around each of next 2 FPDC, sc in each of next 2 sts, cb4, sc in each of next 2 sts, FPDC around each of next 2 FPDC, sc in each of last 2 sts, turn.

Row 7: Ch 1, sc in each of first 2 sts, FPDC around each of next 2 FPDC, sc in each of next 2 sts, FPDC around each of next 4 FPTR, sc in each of next 2 sts, FPDC around each of next 2 FPDC, sc in each of last 2 sts, turn.

Row 9: Ch 1, sc in each of first 2 sts, FPDC around each of next 2 FPDC, sc in each of next 2 sts, cb4, sc in each of next 2 sts, FPDC around each of next 2 FPDC, sc in each of last 2 sts, turn.

Row 11: Ch 1, sc in each of first 2 sts, TW2L, TW2R, TW2L, TW2R, sc in each of last 2 sts, turn.

Note: Sk 4 sc in previous row when working a TW2L followed by a TW2R. (See figure 39, page 91.)

Row 13: Ch 1, sc in each of first 3 sts, cb4R, sc in each of next 2 sts, cb4, sc in each of last 3 sts, turn.

Row 15: Ch 1, sc in each of first 2 sts, TW2R, TW2L using rem 2 post sts of cb4R in row below, TW2R, TW2L over next 3 sts using rem 2 post sts of cb4 in row below, sc in each of last 2 sts, turn.

Row 17 (Dec): Ch 1, sc in each of first 2 sts, FPDC around each of next 2 FPDC, sc in each of next 3 sts, [FPDC around FPDC in row below leaving last 2 lps on hk, FPDC around next FPDC in row below leaving last lp on hk (3 lps on hk), YO, draw through 3 lps on hk, only sk 1 sc in previous row behind post st dec just made (FPDC2tog made)] twice, sc in each of next 3 sts, FPDC around each of next 2 FPDC, sc in each of last 2 sts, turn.

Row 19 (Dec): Ch 1, sc in each of first 2 sts, FPDC around each of next 2 FPDC, sc in each of next 3 sts, [working both FPDC2tog in row below as 1 st, make 1 FPTR leaving last 2 lps on hk, *FPTR around same 2 FPDC2tog in row below leaving last st of this FPTR on hk*, rep from * to * 2 more times, YO, draw through 5 lps on hk, sk only 2 sc in previous row behind post sts just made (FPTR4tog made)], sc in each of next 3 sts, FPDC around each of next 2 FPDC, sc in each of last 2 sts, turn. [15 sts]

Row 21 (Inc): Ch 1, sc in each of first 2 sts, FPDC around each of next 2 FPDC, sc in each of next 2 sts, working all 4 posts of FPTR4tog as 1 st make 4 FPDC, sk 3 sc in previous row behind 4 post sts just made, sc in each of next 2 sts, FPDC around each of next 2 FPDC, sc in each of last 2 sts, turn. [16 sts]

Row 23: Ch 1, sc in each of first 2 sts, TW2L, TW2R, TW2L, TW2R, sc in each of last 2 sts, turn.

Row 25: Ch 1, sc in each of first 3 sts, cb4R, sc in each of next 2 sts, cb4, sc in each of last 3 sts, turn.

Row 27: Ch 1, sc in each of first 2 sts, TW2R, TW2L over next 3 sts using rem 2 posts from cb4 in row below, TW2R over next 3 sts using first 2 (bottom-most) posts from cb4R in row below, TW2L, sc in each of last 2 sts, turn.

Row 29: Ch 1, sc in each of first 2 sts, FPDC around each of next 2 FPDC, sc in each of next 2 sts, cb4, sc in each of next 2 sts, FPDC around each of next 2 FPDC, sc in each of last 2 sts, turn.

ROW 31: Ch 1, sc in each of first 2 sts, FPDC around each of next 2 FPDC, sc in each of next 2 sts, FPDC around each of next 4 FPTR, sc in each of next 2 sts, FPDC around each of next 2 FPDC, sc in each of last 2 sts, turn.

Rows 4–31 form Interlacing Cables panel.

Back

1 • With smaller hk, ch 12.

FOUNDATION ROW: Sc in 2nd ch from hk (count as st) and in each ch to end, turn. [11 sc]

SINGLE CROCHET RIBBING

2 • **ROW 2**: Ch 1, sc blo in first and each st to end, turn.

3 • Rep step 2 (row 2) 66 (70, 76, 82, 86) more times.

BODY

Change to larger hk, pivot to work across one long edge of ribbing and cont as foll:

4 • **ROW 1 (INC; RS)**: Ch 1, 2 sc in end of first row, sc in end of each row to last row, 2 sc in end of last row, turn. [70 (74, 80, 86, 90) sts]

5 • **ROW 2**: Ch 1, sc in each of first 0 (2, 2, 2, 1) sts, pm, sc in each of next 27 (27, 30, 33, 36) sts, pm, sc in each of next 16 sts, pm, sc in each of next 27 (27, 30, 33, 36) sts, pm, sc in next and each st to end, turn.

Note: In foll steps, Extra Small sk right and left borders.

6 • **ROW 3: RIGHT BORDER**: Ch 1, sc in first and each st to marker;

DIAGONAL POSTS RIGHT SLANT SETUP: Sc in next st, FPDC around next sc in row below, *sc in each of next 2 sts, FPDC around next sc in row below*, rep from * to * to last st before marker, sc in next st;

INTERLACING CABLES SETUP: Sc in each of next 2 sts, FPDC around each of next 2 sc in row below, sc in each of next 2 sts, FPDC around each of next 4 sc in row below, sc in each of next 2 sts, FPDC around each of next 2 sc in row below, sc in each of next 2 sts;

DIAGONAL POSTS LEFT SLANT SETUP: Sc in next st, FPDC around next sc in row below, *sc in each of next 2 sts, FPDC around next sc in row below*, rep from * to * to st before marker, sc in next st;

LEFT BORDER: Sc in next and each st to end, turn.

7 • **ROW 4 AND ALL WS ROWS**: Ch 1, sc in first and each st to end.

8 • **ROW 5: RIGHT BORDER**: Sc in first and each st to marker;

DIAGONAL POSTS RIGHT SLANT: Sc in each of next 3 sts, TWR, sc in next st, *TWR, sc in next st*, rep from * to * to last 3 sts before marker, 2 FPDC around next FPDC, sc in last st;

INTERLACING CABLES: Sc in next 2 sts, FPDC around each of next 2 FPDC, sc in each of next 2 sts, cb4, sc in each of next 2 sts, FPDC around each of next 2 FPDC, sc in each of next 2 sts;

DIAGONAL POSTS LEFT SLANT: Sc in next st, 2 FPDC around first FPDC, sc in next st, *TWL, sc in next st*, rep from * to * to last 2 sts before marker, sc in next 2 sts;

LEFT BORDER: Sc in next and each st to end, turn.

9 • Cont even in st patts as established, starting with row 6 of Diagonal Posts Right Slant (see page 10), row 6 of Interlacing Cables (see page 11), and row 6 of Diagonal Posts Left Slant (see page 10), maintaining sc borders for all sizes *except* Extra Small until 24½ (25, 25¾, 26½, 28)" from lower edge of ribbing. Fasten off.

Front

1 • Work as for back, steps 1–9, until 22 (22, 22¾, 23, 24½)" from beg, ending with RS row complete.

RIGHT NECK SHAPING

Cont in borders, st patt, and panel as established, work as foll:

2 • **NEXT ROW (DEC; WS)**: Patt across first 27 (28, 31, 33, 35) sts, sc in next st, sc2tog, turn. Rem sts unworked. [29 (30, 33, 35, 37) sts]

3 • **NEXT ROW (DEC)**: Ch 1, sc2tog, sc in next st, patt as established to end, turn. [28 (29, 32, 34, 36) sts]

NEXT ROW (DEC): Patt as established to last 3 sts, sc in next st, sc2tog, turn. [27 (28, 31, 33, 35) sts]

4 • Rep step 3 (last 2 rows) 3 more times. [21 (22, 25, 27, 29) sts]

5 • Work even in st patts as established until 24½ (25, 25¾, 26½, 28)" from beg. Fasten off.

LEFT NECK SHAPING

6 • With WS facing, working into last full-width row and starting at inner right front shoulder, sk next 10 (12, 12, 14, 14) sts. Join yarn with sc2tog (count as st). Working in border, patts, and panels as established on last full-width row, cont as foll:

NEXT ROW (DEC; WS): Sc in next st, patt as established to end, turn. [29 (30, 33, 35, 37) sts]

7 • **NEXT ROW (DEC):** Patt as established to last 3 sc, sc in next st, sc2tog, turn. [28 (29, 32, 34, 36) sts]

NEXT ROW (DEC): Ch 1, sc2tog, sc in next st, patt as established to end, turn. [27 (28, 31, 33, 35) sts]

8 • Rep step 7 (last 2 rows) 3 more times. [21 (22, 25, 27, 29) sts]

9 • Work even in st patts as established until 24½ (25, 25¾, 26½, 28)" from beg of ribbing. Fasten off.

Sleeve *(Make 2)*

1 • Work as for back, steps 1–3 (Single Crochet Ribbing) until 33 (33, 33, 35, 35) rows complete.

Change to larger hk, pivot to work across one long edge of ribbing and cont as foll:

2 • **ROW 1 (INC; RS):** Ch 1, sc in each of first 1 (1, 1, 2, 2) row ends, pm, sc in next row end, *2 sc in next row end, sc in each of next 3 row ends*, rep from * to * 6 more times, 2 sc in next row end, sc in next row end, pm, sc in each of last 1 (1, 1, 2, 2) row ends, turn. [41 (41, 41, 43, 43) sts]

3 • **ROW 2:** Ch 1, sc in first and each st to end, turn.

4 • **ROW 3 (INC):** Ch 1, 2 sc in first st, sc in each 0 (0, 0, 1, 1) st to marker, *sc in next st, FPDC around next sc in row below, sc in next st*, rep from * to * to marker, sc in next and each st to last st, 2 sc in last st, turn. [43 (43, 43, 45, 45) sts]

5 • **ROWS 4 AND 6:** Ch 1, sc in first and each st to end, turn.

ROW 5: Ch 1, sc in first and each st to marker, *sc in next st, FPDC around next FPDC in row below, sc in next st*, rep from * to * to last st, sc in last st, turn.

ROW 7 (INC): Ch 1 (do not count as st), 2 sc in first st, sc in each st to marker, patt as established to marker, sc in next and each st to last st, 2 sc in last st, turn. [45 (45, 45, 47, 47) sts]

6 • Rep step 5 (last 4 rows) 12 (13, 13, 13, 15) more times. [69 (71, 71, 73, 77) sts]

7 • Work even in st patt as established until 18 (18½, 19, 19½, 20)" from beg of ribbing. Fasten off.

Neckband

1 • Sew back to front at right shoulder.

2 • Place marker on back inner edge of left shoulder 6 (6¼, 7¼, 7¾, 8¼)" from corner.

3 • With smaller hk, RS facing, join yarn with sc (count as st) at inner edge of left front shoulder and work evenly spaced sts along neck edge as foll:

ROW 1 (RS): LEFT FRONT: 9 (11, 11, 13, 13) sc;

FRONT BASE OF NECK: 10 (12, 12, 14, 14) sc;

RIGHT FRONT: 9 (11, 11, 13, 13) sc;

BACK NECK: 26 (28, 28, 30, 30) sc to marker. [54 (62, 62, 70, 70) sts]
Fasten off.

4 • Work as for back, steps 1 and 2 (Single Crochet Ribbing).

5 • Rep last row 52 (60, 60, 68, 68) more times. Fasten off.

Finishing

1 • With RS tog and easing neck edge as necessary, sew one long edge of neckband to neck edging, matching each row end to each st.

2 • Sew front to back at left shoulder and neckband.

3 • Fold top half of neckband inside sweater. Loosely sew long edge to WS of neck edging, matching each row end to each st.

4 • On front and back, pm at each side (vertical edge) 9¾ (10, 10, 10¼, 11)" below shoulder seam. Sew sleeves into body between markers. (See "Inserting Sleeves" on page 93.)

5 • Sew back to front at sides and underarms.

Double Crochet Weave

Climbing Cables

A loose, comfy sweater is ideal for a weekend getaway, and this one is fun to stitch. With a basic front placket and straight sides, it's a great project if you're just learning to shape while working cables. This pull-on garment's namesake is a simple cable stitch pattern that winds its way up the lower body and sleeves of the garment.

YARN

Lambs Pride Superwash from Brown Sheep, color #SW95 Peacock

Extra Small	•	11 balls
Small	•	11 balls
Medium	•	12 balls
Large	•	12 balls
Extra Large	•	13 balls

SUPPLIES

H/8 (5 mm) crochet hook
4 stitch markers

GAUGE

15 sts and 18 rows to 4" in Climbing Cables st patt

15 sts and 12 rows to 4" in Double Crochet Weave st patt

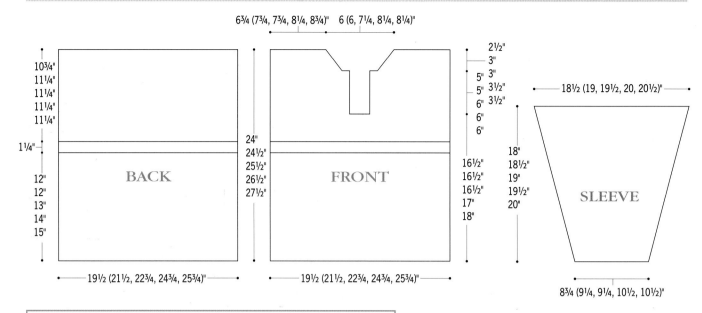

SIZING	Extra Small	Small	Medium	Large	Extra Large
To fit bust	31½"	34¼"	37¼"	41"	43¼"
Finished bust	39"	43"	45½"	49½"	51½"
Shoulder width	6¾"	7¾"	7¾"	8¼"	8¾"
Sleeve length	18½"	19"	19½"	20"	20½"
Center back length	24½"	25"	26"	27"	28"

CLIMBING CABLES STITCH PATTERN

Multiple of 8 sts + 5 sts (add 1 ch for base ch)

FOUNDATION ROW (RS): Sc in 2nd ch from hk (count as st) and in each ch to end, turn.

ROW 2: Ch 1, sc in first and each st to end, turn.

ROW 3: Ch 1, sc in each of first 2 sts, FPDC around next sc in row below (third st from edge or marker), *sc in each of next 2 sts, FPDC around each of next 3 sc in row below (third, fourth, and fifth sts from last FPDC), sc in each of next 2 sts, FPDC around next sc in row below (third st from last FPDC)*, rep from * to * to last 2 sts, sc in each of last 2 sts, turn.

ROWS 4 AND 6: Ch 1, sc in first and each st to end, turn.

ROW 5: Ch 1, sc in each of first 2 sts, FPDC around first FPDC, *sc in each of next 2 sts, cb3, sc in each of next 2 sts, FPDC around next FPDC*, rep from * to * to last 2 sts, sc in each of next 2 sts, turn.

ROW 7: Ch 1, sc in each of first 2 sts, FPDC around next st, *sc in each of next 2 sts, FPDC around each of next 3 sts, sc in each of next 2 sts, FPDC around next st*, rep from * to * to last 2 sts, sc in each of last 2 sts, turn.

Rows 4–7 form Climbing Cables st patt rep.

DOUBLE CROCHET WEAVE STITCH PATTERN

Multiple of 2 sts + 1 st (add 1 ch for base ch)

FOUNDATION ROW (WS): Sc in 2nd ch from hk (count as st) and in each ch to end, turn.

ROW 2: Ch 1, sc in first st, *ch 1, sk next st, sc in next st*, rep from * to * to end, turn.

ROW 3: Ch 2, *dc in sk st in row below by working around previous row without compressing ch st (sdc made), ch 1, sk next st*, rep from * to * to last 2 sts, sdc in next sk st in row below, hdc in last st, turn.

ROW 4: Ch 2, *ch 1, sk next sdc, sdc in next sk st in row below*, rep from * to * to last 2 sts, ch 1, sk next sdc, hdc in last st (top of ch 2), turn.

ROW 5: Ch 2, *sdc in next (sk) sdc in row below, ch 1, sk next sdc*, rep from * to * to last 2 sts, sdc in next sdc in row below, hdc sc in last st, turn.

Rows 4–5 form Double Crochet Weave st patt rep.

Back

1 • Ch 74 (82, 86, 94, 98).

FOUNDATION ROW (RS): Sc in 2nd ch from hk (count as st) and in each ch to end, turn. [73 (81, 85, 93, 97) sts]

LOWER BODY

2 • **ROW 2 (WS):** Ch 1, sc in each st to end, turn.

3 • **ROW 3:** Ch 1, sc in each of first 2 (2, 0, 0, 2) sts, pm, sc in each of next 2 sts, FPDC around next sc in row below, *sc in each of next 2 sts, FPDC around each of next 3 sc in row below, sc in each of next 2 sts, FPDC around next sc in row below*, rep from * to * to last 4 (4, 2, 2, 4) sts, sc in each of next 2 sts, pm, sc in each st to end, turn.

Maintaining sc edge sts (which are outside markers in Extra Small, Small, and Extra Large), cont even in Climbing Cables st patt (see page 16) as established, starting with row 4, until 12 (12, 13, 14, 15)" from beg, ending with RS row complete. Remove markers.

SLANTED POSTS BAND

4 • **NEXT ROW (WS):** Ch 1, sc in first and each st to end, turn.

5 • **NEXT ROW:** Ch 1, sc in each of first 3 sts, *ch 1, sk next st, sc in next st*, rep from * to * to end, turn.

6 • **NEXT ROW:** Ch 1, sc in first and each st and ch-sp to end, turn.

7 • **NEXT ROW:** Ch 1, [insert hk in first st, YO, draw through lp, tr in first sk st in row below, YO, draw through rem 2 lps on hk, do not sk st in previous row (sctr2tog made)], sc in next st, *tr in next sk st in row below, sk st in previous row behind tr just made, sc in next st*, rep from * to * to last 3 sts, sc in each st to end, turn.

8 • **NEXT ROW:** Ch 1, sc in each st to end, turn.

YOKE

9 • **NEXT ROW (RS):** Ch 1, sc in first st, *ch 1, sk next st, sc in next st*, rep from * to * to end, turn.

10 • **NEXT ROW:** Ch 2, sdc (see Double Crochet Weave st patt row 3, page 16, or the stitch entry in "Featured Stitches Guide," figure 26 on page 89) in

first sk st in row below, *ch 1, sk next st, sdc in next sk st in row below*, rep from * to * to last st, hdc in last st, turn.

11 • **NEXT ROW:** Ch 3 (count as hdc and ch 1), sk next sdc, *sdc in next sk st in row below, ch 1, sk next sdc*, rep from * to * to last st, hdc in last st, turn.

12 • Starting with row 5, work even in Double Crochet Weave st patt as established until 23¾ (24¼, 25¼, 26¼, 27¼)" from beg, ending with RS row complete.

13 • **NEXT ROW (FINISHING; WS):** Ch 2, sdc in first sk sdc in row below, *hdc in next sdc, sdc in next sk sdc in row below*, rep from * to * to last st, hdc in last st. Fasten off.

Front

1 • Work as for back until 16½ (16½, 16½, 17, 18)" from beg, ending with RS row complete.

2 • Next Row (Placket; WS): Ch 2, sdc in first sk sdc in row below, *ch 1, sk next sdc, sdc in next sk sdc in row below*, rep from * to * 14 (16, 17, 19, 20) more times, **hdc in next sdc, sdc in next sk sdc in row below**, rep from ** to ** 3 more times, hdc in next sdc, ***sdc in next sk sdc in row below, ch 1, sk next sdc***, rep from *** to *** to last 2 sts, sdc in next sk sdc in row below, hdc in last st, turn.

LEFT FRONT

3 • Next Row (Dec; RS): Ch 3 (count as hdc and ch 1), sk next sdc, sdc in first sdc in row below, *ch 1, sk next sdc, sdc in next sk sdc in row below*, rep from * to * 13 (15, 16, 18, 19) more times, hdc in next sdc, turn. Rem sts unworked. [32 (36, 38, 42, 44) sts]

4 • Next Row: Ch 3 (count as hdc and ch 1), sk first sdc, sdc in first sk sdc in row below, *ch 1, sk next sdc, sdc in next sk sdc in row below*, rep from * to * to last st, hdc in last st, turn.

5 • Rep step 4 (last row) until 21½ (21½, 22½, 23, 24)" from beg, ending with RS row complete.

LEFT NECK SHAPING

6 • Next Row (WS): Ch 2, *hdc in next sdc, sdc in next sk sdc in row below*, rep from * to * 1 (1, 1, 2, 2) more time, **ch 1, sk next sdc in previous row, sdc in next sk sdc of previous row**, rep from ** to ** to last st, hdc in last st, turn.

7 • Next Row (Dec): Ch 3 (count as hdc and ch 1), sk next sdc, sdc in first sdc in row below, *ch 1, sk next sdc, sdc in next sk sdc in row below*, rep from * to * to last 5 (5, 5, 7, 7) sts, [YO, insert hk in next st, YO, draw through lp, insert hk in next st, YO, draw through lp, YO, draw lp through rem 4 lps on hk (left hdc dec made)], turn. Rem sts unworked. [28 (32, 34, 36, 38) sts]

8 • Next Row (Dec): Ch 1, [insert hk in next st, YO, draw through lp, hdc in next st in usual manner, YO, draw through rem 2 lps on hk (right hdc dec

made)], sdc in next sk sdc in row below, *ch 1, sk next sdc, sdc in next sk sdc in row below*, rep from * to * to last st, hdc in last st, turn. [27 (31, 33, 35, 37) sts]

9 • Next Row (Dec): Ch 3 (count as hdc and ch 1), sk first sdc, sdc in first sk sdc in row below, *ch 1, sk next sdc, sdc in next sk sdc in row below*, rep from * to * to last 2 sts, left hdc dec, turn. [26 (30, 32, 34, 36) sts]

Next Row (Dec): Ch 1, right hdc dec, sdc in next sk sdc in row below, *ch 1, sk next sdc, sdc in next sk sdc in row below*, rep from * to * to last st, hdc in last st, turn. [25 (29, 31, 33, 35) sts]

10 • Rep step 9 (last 2 rows) 0 (0, 1, 1, 1) more times. [25 (29, 29, 31, 33) sts]

11 • Starting with row 4 of Double Crochet Weave (see page 16), work even in st patt until 23¾ (24¼, 25¼, 26¼, 27¼)" from beg, ending with RS row complete.

12 • Next Row (Finishing; WS): Ch 2, sdc in first sk sdc in row below, *hdc in next sdc, sdc in next sk sdc in row below*, rep from * to * to last st, hdc in last st. Fasten off.

RIGHT FRONT

13 • With RS facing, working into last full-width row and starting at inner left front shoulder shaping, sk next 9 sts. Join yarn with ch 2 in next sdc (count as hdc). Working in st patt as established on last full-width row, cont as foll:

Next Row (RS): *Sdc in next sk sdc in row below, ch 1, sk next sdc*, rep from * to * to last st, hdc in last st, turn. [32 (36, 38, 42, 44) sts]

14 • Next Row: Ch 2, sdc in first sk sdc in row below, *ch 1, sk next sdc, sdc in next sk sdc in row below*, rep from * to * to last 2 sts, ch 1, sk next sdc, hdc in last st, turn.

15 • Rep step 14 (last row) until 21½ (21½, 22½, 23, 24)" from beg, ending with RS row complete.

RIGHT NECK SHAPING

16 • Next Row (WS): Ch 2, sdc in first sk sdc in row below, *ch 1, sk next sdc, sdc in next sk sdc in row below*, rep from * to * to last 4 (4, 4, 6, 6) sts, **hdc in next sdc, sdc in next sk sdc in row below**, rep from ** to ** 0 (0, 0, 1, 1) more times, hdc in next 2 sts, turn.

17 • NEXT ROW (DEC): Ch 1, sl st in each of next 3 (3, 3, 5, 5) sts (do not count as sts), right hdc dec, *sdc in next sk sdc in row below, ch 1, sk next sdc*, rep from * to * to last st, hdc in last st, turn. [28 (32, 34, 36, 38) sts]

18 • NEXT ROW (DEC): Ch 2, sdc in first sk sdc in row below, *ch 1, sk next sdc, sdc in next sk sdc in row below*, rep from * to * to last 2 sts, left hdc dec, turn. [27 (31, 33, 35, 37) sts]

19 • NEXT ROW (DEC): Ch 1, right hdc dec, *sdc in next sk sdc in row below, ch 1, sk next sdc*, rep from * to * to last st, hdc in last st, turn. [26 (30, 32, 34, 36) sts]

NEXT ROW (DEC): Ch 2, sdc in next sk sdc in row below, *ch 1, sk next sdc, sdc in next sk sdc in row below*, rep from * to * to last 2 sts, left hdc dec, turn. [25 (29, 31, 33, 35) sts]

20 • Rep step 19 (last 2 rows) 0 (0, 1, 1, 1) more times. [25 (29, 29, 31, 33) sts]

21 • Starting with row 4, work even in Double Crochet Weave st patt 23¾ (24¼, 25¼, 26¼, 27¼)" from beg, ending with RS row complete.

22 • NEXT ROW (FINISHING; WS): Ch 2, sdc in first sk sdc in row below, *hdc in next sdc, sdc in next sk sdc in row below*, rep from * to * to last st, hdc in last st. Fasten off.

Sleeve (Make 2)

1 • Ch 34 (36, 36, 40, 40).

FOUNDATION ROW (RS): Sc in 2nd ch from hk (count as st) and in each ch to end. [33 (35, 35, 39, 39) sts]

2 • Row 2: Ch 1, sc in first and each st to end, turn.

3 • Row 3 (INC): Ch 1, 2 sc in first st, sc in each of next 1 (2, 2, 0, 0) st, pm, sc in each of next 2 sts, FPDC around next sc in row below, *sc in each of next 2 sts, FPDC around each of next 3 sc in row below, sc in each of next 2 sts, FPDC around next sc in row below*, rep from * to * to last 4 (5, 5, 3, 3) sts, sc in each of next 2 sts, pm, sc in each st to last st, 2 sc in last st, turn. [35 (37, 37, 41, 41) sts]

4 • Row 4: Ch 1, sc in first and each st to end, turn.

5 • Starting with row 5 of Climbing Cables st patt, work 2 more rows.

6 • NEXT ROW (INC): Ch 1, 2 sc in first st, sc in each st to marker, patt as established to next marker, sc in each st to last st, 2 sc in last st, turn. [37 (39, 39, 43, 43) sts]

Work 3 rows even in st patt as established.

7 • Rep step 6 (last 4 rows) 16 (16, 17, 16, 17) more times. [69 (71, 73, 75, 77) sts]

8 • Work even in st patt as established until 18 (18½, 19, 19½, 20)" from beg. Fasten off.

Back Edging

1 • With RS of back facing, join yarn with sc (count as st) in corner and working into beg ch, sc in each ch to opposite edge, turn.

2 • NEXT ROW (WS): Ch 1, sc in first and each st to end, turn.

NEXT ROW: Ch 1, sl st in first and each st to end. Fasten off.

Front Edging

Work as for back edging.

Cuff Edging

Work as for back edging.

Right Front Placket

1 • With RS of front facing, join yarn with sc (count as st) at bottom of placket opening and work evenly spaced sts as foll:

FOUNDATION ROW (RS): 20 (20, 23, 23, 23) sc up opening to right front neck, turn.

2 • Row 2: Ch 1, sc in first and each st to end, turn.

3 • Row 3 (LACING HOLES; INC): Ch 1, sc in each of first 2 sts, ch 2, sk next st, *sc in each of next 4 (4, 5, 5, 5) sts, ch 2, sk next st*, rep from * to * to last 2 sts, sc in each of last 2 sts, turn. [24 (24, 27, 27, 27)] sts

4 • Row 4 (DEC): Ch 1, sc in each of first 2 sts, sc in next ch-sp, *sc in each of next 4 (4, 5, 5, 5) sts, sc in next ch-sp*, rep from * to * to last 2 sts, sc each of last 2 sts, turn. [20 (20, 23, 23, 23) sts]

5 • Row 5: Ch 1, sc in first and each st to end, turn. Fasten off.

Left Front Placket

1 • With RS of front facing, join yarn with sc (count as st) at top of left front opening (neck edge) and work evenly spaced sts as foll:

FOUNDATION ROW (RS): 20 (20, 23, 23, 23) sc down placket opening to bottom.

2 • As steps 2–5 of right front placket.

Neckband

1 • Sew back to front at both shoulders.

2 • With RS facing, join yarn with sc (count as st) at top of right front (neck edge) in end of last row of placket and work evenly spaced sts as foll:

ROW 1 (RS): RIGHT FRONT NECK BASE: 6 (6, 6, 8, 8) sc;
RIGHT FRONT SLOPE: 8 (10, 10, 12, 12) sc;
BACK NECK: 23 (23, 27, 31, 31) sc;
LEFT FRONT SLOPE: 8 (10, 10, 12, 12) sc;
LEFT FRONT NECK BASE: 7 (7, 7, 9, 9) sc to last row of left front placket, turn. [53 (57, 61, 73, 73) sts]

ROW 2: Ch 1, sc in each of first 0 (2, 0, 2, 2) sts, pm, sc in each st to last 0 (2, 0, 2, 2) sts, pm, sc in each st to end, turn.

3 • Starting with row 3, work even in Climbing Cables st patt between markers (with sc sts outside markers) until 3" from beg. Fasten off.

Assembly

1 • On front and back, place marker at each side (vertical edge) 9¼ (9½, 9¾, 10, 10¼)" below shoulder seams. Sew sleeves into body between markers. (See "Inserting Sleeves" on page 93.)

2 • Sew back to front at sides and underarms.

Placket Lacing

1 • Cut 3 lengths of yarn, each 150" long. Tie lengths tog at one end with overhand knot.

2 • Twist lengths tog tightly. Fold twisted length in half and knot all yarn ends at rem end. Tie another knot 46" from one end. Trim loose yarn ends ¼" beyond knots.

3 • Thread lace back and forth through holes in right and left plackets.

Country Lane

This vest works up quickly and with little effort. It's made with an allover pattern, without post stitches. The basketweave effect is achieved with pairs of double crochet stitches worked diagonally, in opposite directions, across every row. Every two stitches overlap the previous pair to create a cozy, thick fabric.

YARN

Nature Spun Worsted Weight from Brown Sheep
Color A: #N03 Grey Heather

Extra Small	• 6 balls
Small	• 6 balls
Medium	• 6 balls
Large	• 6 balls
Extra Large	• 7 balls

Color B: #110 Blueberry

All Sizes	• 1 ball

SUPPLIES

H/8 (5 mm) crochet hook

26 (26, 26, 28, 28)" separating zipper*

All-purpose sewing thread in color matched to yarn

Hand-sewing needle

Quilter's straight pins (1¼" long, with large head)

Buy the zipper after assembling the garment pieces so that you'll know the exact length required.

GAUGE

20 sts and 9 rows to 4" in Double Basketweave st patt

Double Basketweave

DOUBLE BASKETWEAVE STITCH PATTERN

Multiple of 4 sts + 6 sts (also add 1 ch for base ch)

FOUNDATION ROW (RS): Sc in 2nd ch from hk (count as st) and in each ch to end, turn.

ROW 2: Ch 2, hdc in each of next 2 sts, *sk next 2 sts, dc in each of next 2 sts, working behind 2 dc just made (not around front and back of crocheted fabric) (figure 1) dc in each of 2 sk sts*, rep from * to * to last 3 sts, hdc in each of last 3 sts, turn.

FIG. 1

ROW 3: Ch 2, *sk next 2 sts, dc in each of next 2 sts, working in front of 2 dc just made (not around front and back of crocheted fabric), dc in each of 2 sk sts*, rep from * to * to last st, hdc in last st (tch), turn.

Rows 2–3 form Double Basketweave st patt rep.

Back

1 • With A, ch 91 (99, 107, 115, 123).

FOUNDATION ROW (RS): Sc in 2nd ch from hk (count as st) and in each ch to end, turn. [90 (98, 106, 114, 122) sc]

2 • **ROW 2:** Ch 2, hdc in each of next 2 sts, *sk next 2 sts, dc in each of next 2 sts, working behind 2 dc just made dc in each of 2 sk sts*, rep from * to * to last 3 sts, hdc in each of last 3 sts, turn.

3 • **ROW 3:** Ch 2, *sk next 2 sts, dc in each of next 2 sts, working in front of 2 dc just made dc in each of 2 sk sts*, rep from * to * to last st, hdc in last st, turn.

4 • Cont even in Double Basketweave st patt as established (rep steps 2 and 3, last 2 rows) until 15½ (15½, 16, 16, 16½)" from beg, ending with WS row complete.

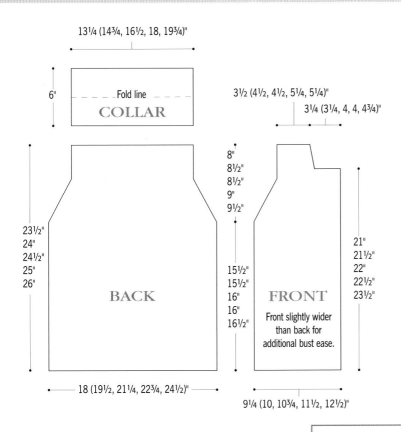

13¼ (14¾, 16½, 18, 19¾)"

6"

Fold line

COLLAR

3½ (4½, 4½, 5¼, 5¼)"

3¼ (3¼, 4, 4, 4¾)"

8"
8½"
8½"
9"
9½"

23½"
24"
24½"
25"
26"

15½"
15½"
16"
16"
16½"

BACK

21"
21½"
22"
22½"
23½"

FRONT

Front slightly wider
than back for
additional bust ease.

18 (19½, 21¼, 22¾, 24½)"

9¼ (10, 10¾, 11½, 12½)"

▓ SIZING	Extra Small	Small	Medium	Large	Extra Large
To fit bust	31½"	34¼"	37¼"	41"	43¼"
Finished bust	36½"	39½"	42¾"	45¾"	49½"
Shoulder width	3½"	4½"	4½"	5¼"	5¼"
*Center back length**	24½"	25"	25½"	26"	27"

*Measurement from bottom of edging to base of neck. Neckband finished
depth (3") is not included.*

ARMHOLE SHAPING

5 • Next Row (Dec; RS): Ch 1, sl st in each of first
2 sts (do not count as sts), [insert hk in next st, YO,
draw through lp, hdc in next st in usual manner, YO,
draw through rem 2 lps on hk (right hdc dec made)],
hdc in next st, *sk next 2 sts, dc in each of next 2 sts,
working in front of 2 dc just made dc in each of 2 sk
sts*, rep from * to * to last 5 sts, hdc in next st, [YO,
insert hk in next st, YO, draw through lp, insert hk
in next st, YO, draw through lp, YO, draw lp
through rem 4 lps on hk (left hdc dec made)], turn.
Rem 2 sts unworked. [84 (92, 100, 108, 116) sts]

6 • Next Row (Dec): Ch 1, right hdc dec, hdc in
each of next 2 sts, patt as established to last 4 sts, hdc
in each of next 2 sts, left hdc dec, turn. [82 (90, 98,
106, 114) sts]

Next Row (Dec): Ch 1, right hdc dec, hdc in each of
next 3 sts, patt as established to last 5 sts, hdc in
each of next 3 sts, left hdc dec, turn. [80 (88, 96, 104,
112) sts]

Next Row (Dec): Ch 1, right hdc dec, patt as established to last 2 sts, left hdc dec, turn. [78 (86, 94, 102,
110) sts]

Next Row (Dec): Ch 1, right hdc dec, hdc in next st,
patt as established to last 3 sts, hdc in next st, left
hdc dec, turn. [76 (84, 92, 100, 108) sts]

7 • Rep step 6 (last 4 rows) once more. [68 (76, 84,
92, 100) sts]

8 • Next Row (Dec): Ch 1, right hdc dec, hdc in
each of next 2 sts, patt as established to last 4 sts,
hdc in each of next 2 sts, left hdc dec, turn. [66 (74,
82, 90, 98) sts]

9 • Work even in st patt (starting with row 3)
until 23½ (24, 24½, 25, 26)" from beg.
Fasten off.

Left Front

1 • With A, ch 47 (51, 55, 59, 63).

FOUNDATION ROW (RS): Sc in 2nd ch from hk (count as st) and in each ch to end, turn. [46 (50, 54, 58, 62) sc]

2 • Work as for back, starting with step 2, to armhole shaping.

ARMHOLE SHAPING

3 • NEXT ROW (DEC; RS): Ch 1, sl st in each of first 2 sts (do not count as sts), right hdc dec, hdc in next st, patt as established to last st, hdc in last st, turn. [43 (47, 51, 55, 59) sc]

4 • NEXT ROW (DEC): Ch 2, hdc in each of next 2 sts, patt as established to last 4 sts, hdc in each of next 2 sts, left hdc dec, turn. [42 (46, 50, 54, 58) sts]

5 • NEXT ROW (DEC): Ch 1, right hdc dec, hdc in each of next 3 sts, patt as established to last 3 sts, hdc in each of last 3 sts, turn. [41 (45, 49, 53, 57) sts]

NEXT ROW (DEC): Ch 2, hdc in each of next 2 sts, patt as established to last 2 sts, left hdc dec, turn. [40 (44, 48, 52, 56) sts]

NEXT ROW (DEC): Ch 1, right hdc dec, hdc in next st, patt as established to last 3 sts, hdc in each of last 3 sts, turn. [39 (43, 47, 51, 55) sts]

6 • Rep steps 4 and 5 (last 4 rows) once more. [35 (39, 43, 47, 51) sts]

7 • Rep step 4 once more. [34 (38, 42, 46, 50) sts]

8 • Work even in st patt as established until 21 (21½, 22, 22½, 23½)" from beg, ending with WS row complete.

LEFT NECK SHAPING

9 • NEXT ROW (DEC; RS): Patt as established to last 13 (13, 17, 17, 21) sts, hdc in next st, left hdc dec, turn. Rem 10 (10, 14, 14, 18) sts unworked. [23 (27, 27, 31, 31) sts]

10 • NEXT ROW (DEC): Ch 1, right hdc dec, hdc in each of next 2 sts, patt as established to last 3 sts, hdc in each of last 3 sts, turn. [22 (26, 26, 30, 30) sts]

11 • NEXT ROW (DEC): Patt as established to last 5 sts, hdc in each of next 3 sts, left hdc dec, turn. [21 (25, 25, 29, 29) sts]

12 • NEXT ROW (DEC): Ch 1, right hdc dec, patt as established to last 3 sts, hdc in each of last 3 sts, turn. [20 (24, 24, 28, 28) sts]

13 • NEXT ROW (DEC): Patt as established to last 3 sts, hdc in next st, left hdc dec, turn. [19 (23, 23, 27, 27) sts]

14 • NEXT ROW (DEC): Ch 1, right hdc dec, hdc in each of next 2 sts, patt as established to last 3 sts, hdc in each of last 3 sts, turn. [18 (22, 22, 26, 26) sts] Fasten off.

Right Front

1 • With A, ch 47 (51, 55, 59, 63).

FOUNDATION ROW (RS): Sc in 2nd ch from hk (count as st) and in each ch to end, turn. [46 (50, 54, 58, 62) sc]

2 • Work as for back, starting with step 2, to armhole shaping.

ARMHOLE SHAPING

3 • NEXT ROW (DEC; RS): Patt as established to last 5 sts, hdc in next st, left hdc dec, turn. Rem 2 sts unworked. [43 (47, 51, 55, 59) sc]

4 • NEXT ROW (DEC): Ch 1, right hdc dec, hdc in each of next 2 sts, patt as established to last 3 sts, hdc in each of last 3 sts, turn. [42 (46, 50, 54, 58) sts]

5 • NEXT ROW (DEC): Patt as established to last 5 sts, hdc in each of next 3 sts, left hdc dec, turn. [41 (45, 49, 53, 57) sts]

NEXT ROW (DEC): Ch 1, right hdc dec, patt as established to last 3 sts, hdc in each of last 3 sts, turn. [40 (44, 48, 52, 56) sts]

NEXT ROW (DEC): Patt as established to last 3 sts, hdc in next st, left hdc dec, turn. [39 (43, 47, 51, 55) sts]

6 • Rep steps 4 and 5 (last 4 rows) once more. [35 (39, 43, 47, 51) sts]

7 • Rep step 4 once more. [34 (38, 42, 46, 50) sts]

8 • Work even in st patt as established until 21 (21½, 22, 22½, 23½)" from beg, ending with WS row complete.

RIGHT NECK SHAPING

9 • NEXT ROW (DEC; RS): Ch 1, sl st in each of next 10 (10, 14, 14, 18) sts (do not count as sts), right hdc dec, hdc in next st, patt as established to last st, hdc in last st, turn. [23 (27, 27, 31, 31) sts]

10 • NEXT ROW (DEC): Ch 2, hdc in each of next 2 sts, patt as established to last 4 sts, hdc in each of next 2 sts, left hdc dec, turn. [22 (26, 26, 30, 30) sts]

11 • NEXT ROW (DEC): Ch 1, right hdc dec, hdc in each of next 3 sts, patt as established to last st, hdc in last st, turn. [21 (25, 25, 29, 29) sts]

12 • NEXT ROW (DEC): Ch 2, hdc in each of next 2 sts, patt as established to last 2 sts, left hdc dec, turn. [20 (24, 24, 28, 28) sts]

13 • NEXT ROW (DEC): Ch 1 (do not count as st), right hdc dec, hdc in next st, patt as established to last st, hdc in last st, turn. [19 (23, 23, 27, 27) sts]

14 • NEXT ROW (DEC): Ch 2, hdc in each of next 2 sts, patt as established to last 4 sts, hdc in each of next 2 sts, left hdc dec, turn. [18 (22, 22, 26, 26) sts] Fasten off.

Neckband

1 • Sew back to front at shoulders and sides.

2 • With RS facing, join A with sc (count as st) at center front of right front neck edge and work evenly spaced sts as foll:

ROW 1 (RS): RIGHT FRONT NECK BASE: 9 (9, 13, 13, 17) sc;

RIGHT FRONT NECK SLOPE: 8 sc;

BACK NECK: 25 (25, 29, 29, 35) sc;

LEFT FRONT NECK SLOPE: 8 sc;

LEFT FRONT NECK BASE: 10 (10, 14, 14, 18) sc, turn. [61 (61, 73, 73, 87) sts]

3 • ROW 2: Ch 1, sc in first and each st to end, turn.

4 • ROW 3: Ch 1, sc in first st, *FPDC around next sc in row below (second st from edge or last FPDC), sc in next st*, rep from * to * to end, turn.

5 • ROW 4: Ch 1, sc in each st to end, turn.

ROW 5: Ch 1, sc in first st, *FPDC around next FPDC

in row below, sc in next st*, rep from * to * to end, turn.

6 • Rep step 5 (last 2 rows) until 6" from beg. Fasten off. Fold neckband in half to inside and sew loose long edge to first row of neckband.

Body Edging

1 • RS facing, join A with sc (count as st) at center front, upper (folded) edge of neckband and work evenly spaced sts as foll:

2 • ROW 1 (RS): Sc down left front edge, around bottom edge to right front, and up right front edge to top (folded edge) of neckband. Fasten off. Do not turn.

3 • ROW 2 (RS): Join B with sc (count as st) in first st of row 1, sc in next and each st to end, do not turn.

ROW 3 (RS): Ch 1 (do not count as st), rsc in first st and each st to end. Fasten off.

Armhole Edging

1 • With RS facing and beg at one underarm, join A with sc at top of side seam (count as st) and cont as foll:

ROW 1 (RS): Work evenly spaced sc around armhole edge. Fasten off.

2 • Work as for body edging, step 3 (rows 2 and 3). Fasten off.

Finishing

Insert zipper in front opening. (See "Inserting a Zipper" on page 93.)

*Colored
Pebbles*

Maids in a Row

Featuring repeating bands of simple stitch repeats, this sweater is a stunning project for a crocheter with intermediate skills. The sporty style incorporates a little color, which is mixed with cables and texture. The overall effect is well-suited for a man with traditional tastes, yet merely switching the yarn colors can shift the garment to a feminine point of view.

YARN

Naturelle Aran 10 Ply from Naturally Yarns, colors #151 Beige, #154 Black, #158 Brown

Yarn Color	Women's	Men's
A	Beige	Brown
B	Black	Black
C	Brown	Beige

Color A

Woman's Extra Small	8 balls
Woman's Small/ Man's Extra Small	9 balls
Woman's Medium/ Man's Small	9 balls
Woman's Large/ Man's Medium	10 balls
Woman's Extra Large/ Man's Large	10 balls
Woman's 2XL/ Man's Extra Large	11 balls
Woman's 3XL/ Man's 2XL	11 balls

Yarn continued on the next page.

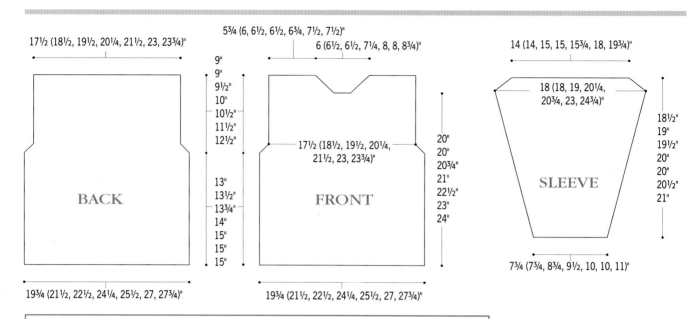

17½ (18½, 19½, 20¼, 21½, 23, 23¾)"

BACK

19¾ (21½, 22½, 24¼, 25½, 27, 27¾)"

5¾ (6, 6½, 6½, 6¾, 7½, 7½)"

6 (6½, 6½, 7¼, 8, 8, 8¾)"

9"
9"
9½"
10"
10½"
11½"
12½"

17½ (18½, 19½, 20¼, 21½, 23, 23¾)"

13"
13½"
13¾"
14"
15"
15"
15"

FRONT

20"
20"
20¾"
21"
22½"
23"
24"

19¾ (21½, 22½, 24¼, 25½, 27, 27¾)"

14 (14, 15, 15, 15¾, 18, 19¾)"

18 (18, 19, 20¼, 20¾, 23, 24¾)"

SLEEVE

18½"
19"
19½"
20"
20"
20½"
21"

7¾ (7¾, 8¾, 9½, 10, 10, 11)"

SIZING

	Extra Small	Small	Medium	Large	Extra Large	2XL	3XL
Women's sizes	Extra Small	Small	Medium	Large	Extra Large	2XL	3XL
Men's sizes		Extra Small	Small	Medium	Large	Extra Large	2XL
To fit bust	31½"	34¼"	37¼"	41"	43¼"	46"	48"
Finished bust	39½"	43"	45"	48½"	51"	54"	55½"
Shoulder width	5¾"	6"	6½"	6½"	6¾"	7½"	7½"
Sleeve length	19"	19½"	20"	20½"	20½"	21"	21½"
Center back length*	22½"	23"	23¾"	24½"	26"	27"	28"

Measurement from bottom of edging to top of back.

Color B

Woman's Extra Small	• 1 ball
Woman's Small/Man's Extra Small	• 1 ball
Woman's Medium/Man's Small	• 1 ball
Woman's Large/Man's Medium	• 2 balls
Woman's Extra Large/Man's Large	• 2 balls
Woman's 2XL/Man's Extra Large	• 2 balls
Woman's 3XL/Man's 2XL	• 2 balls

Color C

All Sizes • 2 balls

SUPPLIES

7 (4.5 mm) crochet hook

2 stitch markers

GAUGE

14 sts to 4" and 14 rows to 3" in Maids in a Row band

COLORED PEBBLES BAND

Multiple of 2 sts + 1 st (also add 1 ch for base ch)

FOUNDATION ROW (RS): With A, sc in 2nd ch from hk (count as st) and in each ch to end, turn.

ROW 2: Ch 1, sc in each st to end, turn.

ROW 3: With B, ch 1, sc in each st to end, turn.

ROW 4: With C, ch 1, sc in each st to end, turn.

ROW 5: With A, ch 1, sc in each st to end, turn.

ROW 6: With C, ch 1, sc in first st, *hdc in next st, sl st loosely in next st*, rep from * to * to last 2 sts, hdc in next st, sc in last st, turn.

ROW 7: With A, ch 1, sc in each of first 2 sts, *ssc in next st, sc in next st*, rep from * to * to last st, sc in last st, turn.

ROW 8: With C, ch 1, sc in each st to end, turn.

ROW 9: With B, ch 1, sc in each st to end, turn.

ROW 10: With A, ch 1, sc in each st to end, turn.

MAIDS IN A ROW BAND

Multiple of 6 sts + 7 sts (also add 1 ch for base ch)

FOUNDATION ROW (RS): Sc in 2nd ch from hk (count as st) and in each ch to end, turn.

Row 2: Ch 1, sc in first and each st to end, turn.

Row 3: Ch 1, sc in each of first 3 sts, *ch 1, sk next st, sc in each of next 5 sts*, rep from * to * to last 4 sts, ch 1, sk next st, sc in each of last 3 sts, turn.

Row 4: Ch 1, sc in first and each st and ch-sp to end, turn.

Row 5: Ch 1, sc in each of first 2 sts, *working in front of crocheted fabric make 3 dc in sk st in row below, sk 3 sc behind 3 dc just made, sc in each of next 3 sts*, rep from * to * to last 5 sts, 3 dc in sk st in row below, sk 3 sc behind 3 dc just made, sc in each of last 2 sts, turn.

Rows 6, 8, 10, 12, and 14: Ch 1, sc in first and each st to end, turn.

Row 7: Ch 1, sc in each of first 2 sts, *cb3 in 3 dc from row 5, sc in each of next 3 sts*, rep from * to * to last 5 sts, cb3, sc in each of last 2 sts, turn.

Rows 9 and 11: Ch 1, sc in each of first 2 sts, *cb3, sc in each of next 3 sts*, rep from * to * to last 5 sts, cb3, sc in each of last 2 sts, turn.

Row 13: Ch 1, sc in each of first 3 sts, *[FPDC around FPDC in row below, leaving last 2 lps on hk, **FPDC around next FPDC in row below, leaving last stitch of this FPDC on hk**, rep from ** to ** once more, YO, draw through rem 4 lps on hk, sk only 1 sc behind post st dec just made (FPDC3tog made)], sc in each of next 5 sts*, rep from * to * to last 4 sts, FPDC3tog, sc in each of last 3 sts, turn.

Back

1 • With A, ch 70 (76, 80, 86, 90, 96, 98).

FOUNDATION ROW (RS): Sc in 2nd ch from hk (count as st) and in each ch to end, turn. [69 (75, 79, 85, 89, 95, 97) sts]

COLORED PEBBLES BAND

2 • ROW 2 (WS): Ch 1, sc in first and each st to end, turn.

3 • ROW 3: With B, ch 1, sc in first and each st to end, turn.

4 • ROW 4: With C, ch 1, sc in each st to end, turn.

5 • ROW 5: With A, ch 1, sc in each st to end, turn.

6 • ROW 6: With C, ch 1, sc in first st, *hdc in next st, sl st loosely in next st*, rep from * to * to last 2 sts, hdc in next st, sc in last st, turn.

7 • ROW 7: With A, ch 1, sc in each of first 2 sts, *ssc in next st, sc in next st*, rep from * to * to last st, sc in last st, turn.

8 • ROW 8: With C, ch 1, sc in each st to end, turn.

9 • ROW 9: With B, ch 1, sc in each st to end, turn.

10 • ROW 10: With A, ch 1, sc in first and each st to end, turn.

MAIDS IN A ROW BAND

11 • ROW 11 (RS): Ch 1, sc in first 1 (1, 0, 0, 2, 2, 0) st, pm, sc in next 3 sts, *ch 1, sk next st, sc in each of next 5 sts*, rep from * to * to last 5 (5, 4, 4, 6, 6, 4) sts, ch 1, sk next st, sc in each of next 3 sts, pm, sc in last 1 (1, 0, 0, 2, 2, 0) st, turn.

12 • Cont in Maids in a Row band as established between markers, working Maids in a Row band rows 4–13 (see column at left) once.

13 • Cont working even, alternating Colored Pebbles band (steps 2–10) and Maids in a Row band (steps 11–12) until 13 (13½, 13¾, 14, 15, 15, 15)" from beg, ending with WS row complete.

ARMHOLE SHAPING

Working in alternating Colored Pebbles and Maids in a Row bands as established, cont as foll:

14 • NEXT ROW (DEC; RS): Patt as established to last st, turn. Rem st unworked. [68 (74, 78, 84, 88, 94, 96) sts]

15 • NEXT ROW (DEC): Ch 1, sc2tog, sc in next st, patt as established to last 3 sts, sc2tog, turn. Rem st unworked. [65 (71, 75, 81, 85, 91, 93) sts]

16 • NEXT ROW (DEC): Ch 1, sc2tog, sc in next st, patt as established to last 3 sts, sc in next st, sc2tog, turn. [63 (69, 73, 79, 83, 89, 91) sts]

17 • Rep step 16 (last row) 1 (2, 2, 4, 4, 4, 4) more time. [61 (65, 69, 71, 75, 81, 83) sts]

18 • Cont even, alternating Colored Pebbles and Maids in a Row bands as established, until 22 (22½, 23¼, 24, 25½, 26½, 27½)" from beg. Fasten off.

Front

1 • Work as for back, steps 1–18, until 20 (20, 20¾, 21, 22½, 23, 24)" from beg, ending with WS row complete.

LEFT NECK SHAPING
Cont alternating Colored Pebbles and Maids in a Row bands as established, work as foll:

2 • NEXT ROW (DEC; RS): Patt as established across first 24 (25, 27, 29, 30, 32, 32) sts, sc in next st, sc2tog, turn. Rem sts unworked. [26 (27, 29, 31, 32, 34, 34) sts]

3 • NEXT ROW (DEC): Ch 1, sc2tog, sc in next st, patt as established to end, turn. [25 (26, 28, 30, 31, 33, 33) sts]

NEXT ROW (DEC): Patt as established to last 3 sts, sc in next st, sc2tog, turn. [24 (25, 27, 29, 30, 32, 32) sts]

4 • Rep step 3 (last 2 rows) 2 (2, 2, 3, 3, 3, 3) more times. [20 (21, 23, 23, 24, 26, 26) sts]

5 • Cont even, alternating Colored Pebbles and Maids in a Row bands as established, until 22 (22½, 23¼, 24, 25½, 26½, 27½)" from beg. Fasten off.

RIGHT NECK SHAPING
Cont alternating Colored Pebbles and Maids in a Row bands as established, work as foll:

6 • With RS facing, working into last full-width row and starting at inner edge of left front shoulder shaping, sk next 7 (9, 9, 7, 9, 11, 13) sts. Join yarn with sc2tog. Working in patt as previously established on last full-width row, cont as foll:

NEXT ROW (RS): Sc in next st, patt as established to end, turn. [26 (27, 29, 31, 32, 34, 34) sts]

7 • NEXT ROW (DEC): Patt as established to last 3 sc, sc in next st, sc2tog, turn. [25 (26, 28, 30, 31, 33, 33) sts]

NEXT ROW (DEC): Ch 1, sc2tog, sc in next st, patt as established to end, turn. [24 (25, 27, 29, 30, 32, 32) sts]

8 • Rep step 7 (last 2 rows) 2 (2, 2, 3, 3, 3, 3) more times. [20 (21, 23, 23, 24, 26, 26) sts]

9 • Work even in patt as established until 22 (22½, 23¼, 24, 25½, 26½, 27½)" from beg. Fasten off.

Sleeve (Make 2)

1 • With A, ch 28 (28, 32, 34, 36, 36, 40).

FOUNDATION ROW (RS): Sc in 2nd ch from hk (count as st) and in each ch to end, turn. [27 (27, 31, 33, 35, 35, 39) sts]

COLORED PEBBLES BAND

2 • ROW 2 (INC; WS) With A, ch 1, 2 sc in first st, sc in each st to last st, 2 sc in last st, turn. [29 (29, 33, 35, 37, 37, 41) sts]

3 • ROW 3: With B, ch 1, sc in each of first 2 (2, 1, 2, 3, 3, 2) sts, pm, sc in each st to last 2 (2, 1, 2, 3, 3, 2) sts, pm, sc in each st to end, turn.

Work in Colored Pebbles band as established (starting with row 4 of back, see page 28), then alternate with Maids in a Row band (rows 3–13), AT THE SAME TIME cont as foll:

4 • ROW 4 (INC): Ch 1, 2 sc in first st, patt as established to last st, 2 sc in last st, turn. [31 (31, 35, 37, 39, 39, 43) sts]

ROW 5: Ch 1, patt as established to end, turn.

5 • Rep step 4 (last 2 rows) 2 (2, 0, 1, 2, 9, 11) more times. [35 (35, 35, 39, 43, 57, 65) sts]

6 • Work 2 rows even in patt as established.

7 • NEXT ROW (INC): Ch 1, 2 sc in first st, patt as established to last st, 2 sc in last st, turn. [37 (37, 37, 41, 45, 59, 67) sts]

Work 3 rows even in patt as established.

8 • Rep step 7 (last 4 rows) 13 (13, 15, 15, 14, 11, 10) more times. [63 (63, 67, 71, 73, 81, 87) sts]

9 • Work even in patt as established until 17 (17½, 18, 18, 18, 18½, 19)", ending with WS row complete.

SLEEVE CAP
Cont alternating Colored Pebbles and Maids in a Row bands as established, work as foll:

10 • NEXT ROW (DEC; RS): Patt as established to last st, turn. Rem st unworked. [62 (62, 66, 70, 72, 80, 86) sts]

11 • NEXT ROW (DEC): Ch 1, sc2tog, patt as established to last 3 sts, sc2tog, turn. Rem st unworked. [59 (59, 63, 67, 69, 77, 83) sts]

12 • NEXT ROW (DEC): Ch 1, sc2tog, patt as established to last 2 sts, sc2tog, turn. [57 (57, 61, 65, 67, 75, 81) sts]

13 • Rep step 12 (last row) 4 (4, 4, 6, 6, 6, 6) more times. [49 (49, 53, 53, 55, 63, 69) sts] Fasten off.

Back Edging

1 • With RS of back facing, join A with sc (count as st) in bottom corner and cont as foll:

ROW 1 (RS): Sc 55 (59, 63, 67, 71, 75, 77) sts evenly across bottom edge, do not turn.

2 • NEXT ROW (RS): Ch 1 (do not count as st), rsc in first st to right, rsc in each sc to end. Fasten off.

Front Edging

Work as for back edging.

Sleeve Edging

With RS facing, join A with sc (count as st) in corner of wrist and cont as foll:

ROW 1 (RS): Sc 21 (21, 25, 27, 29, 29, 31) sts evenly across bottom edge, do not turn.

NEXT ROW (RS): With B, ch 1 (do not count as st), rsc in first st to the right, rsc in each sc to end. Fasten off.

Neckband

1 • Sew back to front at right shoulder.

2 • Mark inner edge of left shoulder on front with marker 5¾ (6, 6½, 6½, 6¾, 7½, 7½)" from edge. Mark inside corner of left shoulder on back in same manner.

3 • With A and RS facing, join yarn with sc (count as st) at marker on front and work evenly spaced sts as foll:

ROW 1 (RS): LEFT FRONT SLOPE: 8 (10, 10, 12, 12, 14, 14) sc;

FRONT NECK BASE: 7 (9, 9, 7, 9, 11, 13) sc;
RIGHT FRONT SLOPE: 9 (11, 11, 13, 13, 15, 15) sc;
BACK NECK: 16 (18, 18, 18, 20, 22, 24) sc, turn. [41 (49, 49, 51, 55, 63, 67) sts]

4 • ROW 2: Ch 1, sc in first and each st to end, turn.

5 • Work Colored Pebbles band, steps 3–10. Remove markers.

6 • NEXT ROW (RS): With A, ch 1, sc in first and each st to end, do not turn.

7 • NEXT ROW (RS): Ch 1, rsc in first st to the right, rsc in each sc to end. Fasten off.

Finishing

1 • Sew left shoulder and collar.

2 • Sew sleeves into body, centering the top of each sleeve on a shoulder seam.

3 • Sew back to front at sides and underarms.

Repeating Cables

Share your quiet time with a sweater that's comfortable to wear and easy to stitch. All of the garment pieces are worked in a three-stitch cable on a background of single crochet stitches. It will only take working a handful of rows to familiarize yourself with the stitch pattern, making this an ideal project to work on whenever you have a free moment. The body is cropped at the high hip. The sleeve has a shaped cap that's set in to the armhole. The high neckband is a stand-up collar that's worked in the same stitch pattern as the body.

YARN

220 from Cascade, color #9447 Forest Green

Extra Small	•	8 balls
Small	•	9 balls
Medium	•	9 balls
Large	•	10 balls
Extra Large	•	11 balls

SUPPLIES

H/8 (5 mm) crochet hook
2 stitch markers

GAUGE

14 sts and 18 rows to 4" in Repeating Cables st patt

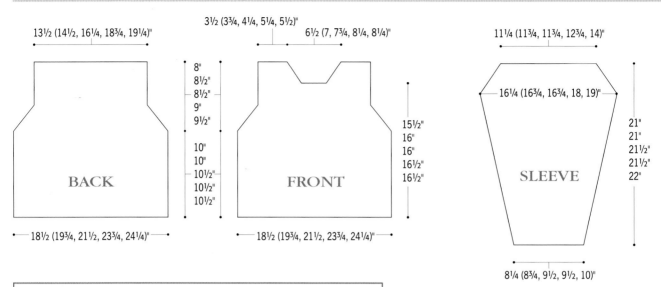

SIZING	Extra Small	Small	Medium	Large	Extra Large
To fit bust	31½"	34¼"	37¼"	41"	43¼"
Finished bust	37"	39½"	43"	47½"	48½"
Shoulder width	3½"	3¾"	4¼"	5¼"	5½"
Sleeve length	21"	21"	21½"	21½"	22"
Center back length	18"	18½"	19"	19½"	20"

REPEATING CABLES STITCH PATTERN

Multiple of 6 sts + 3 st (also add 1 ch for base ch)

FOUNDATION ROW (WS): Sc in 2nd ch from hk (count as st) and in each ch to end, turn.

Row 2: Ch 1, sc in first and each st to end, turn.

Row 3: Ch 1, sc in first and each st to end, turn.

Row 4: Ch 1, sc in each of first 3 sts, *FPDC around each of next 3 sc in row below (starting with fourth st from edge or last FPDC), sc in each of next 3 sts*, rep from * to * to end, turn.

Rows 5 AND 7: Ch 1, sc in first and each st to end, turn.

Row 6: Ch 1, sc in each of first 3 sts, *cb3, sc in each of next 3 sts*, rep from * to * to end, turn.

Row 8: Ch 1, sc in each of first 3 sts, *FPDC around each of next 3 sts, sc in each of next 3 sts*, rep from * to * to end, turn.

Rows 5–8 form Repeating Cables st patt rep.

Back

1 • Ch 66 (70, 76, 84, 86).

FOUNDATION ROW (WS): Sc in 2nd ch from hk (count as st) and in each ch to end, turn. [65 (69, 75, 83, 85) sts]

2 • ROWS 2 AND 3: Ch 1, sc in first and each st to end, turn.

3 • ROW 4: Ch 1, sc in first 1 (0, 0, 1, 2) st, pm, sc in each of next 3 sts, *FPDC around each of next 3 sc in row below, sc in each of next 3 sts*, rep from * to * to last 1 (0, 0, 1, 2) st, pm, sc in each st to end, turn.

4 • ROW 5: Ch 1, sc in first and each st to end, turn.

5 • ROW 6: Ch 1, sc in first and each st to marker, sc in each of next 3 sts, *cb3, sc in each of next 3 sts*, rep from * to * to marker, sc in each st to end, turn.

6 • ROW 7: Ch 1, sc in first and each st to end, turn.

7 • ROW 8: Ch 1, sc in first and each st to marker, sc in each of next 3 sts, *FPDC around each of next 3 sts, sc in each of next 3 sts*, rep from * to * to marker, sc in each st to end, turn.

8 • Maintaining sc edge sts (which are outside markers in Extra Small, Large, and Extra Large), cont even in Repeating Cables st patt as established between markers (rep steps 4–7) until 10 (10, 10½, 10½, 10½)" from beg, ending with WS row complete.

ARMHOLE SHAPING

9 • NEXT ROW (DEC; RS): Remove second marker, ch 1, sc in first and each st to marker, patt as established to last 7 (6, 6, 7, 8) sts, pm, sc in each of next 5 (4, 4, 5, 6) sts, turn. Rem sts unworked. [63 (67, 73, 81, 83) sts]

10 • NEXT ROW (DEC): Remove second marker, ch 1, sc in first and each st to marker, patt as established to last 7 (6, 6, 7, 8) sts, pm, sc in each of next 5 (4, 4, 5, 6) sts, turn. Rem sts unworked. [61 (65, 71, 79, 81) sts]

11 • NEXT ROW (DEC): Ch 1, sc2tog, sc in each st to marker, patt as established to next marker, sc in each st to last 2 sts, sc2tog, turn. [59 (63, 69, 77, 79) sts]

NEXT ROW: Ch 1, sc in first st, patt as established to last st, sc in last st, turn.

12 • Rep step 11 (last 2 rows) 6 more times, moving st markers in 1 full st patt rep at each edge when 1 st rem outside markers. [47 (51, 57, 65, 67) sts]

13 • Cont even in st patt as established until 18 (18½, 19, 19½, 20)" from beg. Fasten off.

Front

1 • Work as for back to step 13.

2 • Cont even in st patt as established until 15½ (16, 16, 16½, 16½)" from beg, ending with RS row complete.

RIGHT NECK SHAPING

3 • NEXT ROW (DEC; WS): Ch 1, sc in each of first 1 (0, 0, 1, 2) st, move marker to current row, patt as established on next 15 (15, 21, 21, 21) sts, pm, sc in each of next 1 (3, 1, 3, 3) st, sc2tog, turn. Rem sts unworked. [18 (19, 23, 26, 27) sts]

Note: Move in marker at neck edge 1 full patt rep (6 sts) when 1 st rem outside marker.

4 • NEXT ROW (DEC): Ch 1, sc2tog, sc in each st to marker, patt as established to next marker, sc in each st to end, turn. [17 (18, 22, 25, 26) sts]

NEXT ROW (DEC): Ch 1, sc in first and each st to marker, patt as established to next marker, sc in each st to last 2 sts, sc2tog, turn. [16 (17, 21, 24, 25) sts]

5 • Rep step 4 (last 2 rows) 2 (2, 3, 3, 3) more times. [12 (13, 15, 18, 19) sts]

6 • Work even in st patt as established until 18 (18½, 19, 19½, 20)" from beg. Fasten off.

LEFT NECK SHAPING

7 • With WS facing, working into last full-width row and starting at inner right front shoulder, sk next 9 (11, 9, 11, 11) sts and join yarn with sc2tog (count as st). Working in st patt as established on last full-width row, cont as foll:

NEXT ROW (WS): Sc in each of next 1 (3, 1, 3, 3) st, pm, patt as established over next 15 (15, 21, 21, 21) sts, pm, sc in each of last 1 (0, 0, 1, 2) st, turn. [18 (19, 23, 26, 27 sts]

Note: Move in marker at neck edge 1 full patt rep (6 sts) when 1 st rem outside marker.

8 • NEXT ROW (DEC): Ch 1, sc in first and each st to marker, patt as established to next marker, sc in each st to last 2 sts, sc2tog, turn. [17 (18, 22, 25, 26) sts]

NEXT ROW (DEC): Ch 1, sc2tog, sc in each st to marker, patt as established to next marker, sc in each st to end, turn. [16 (17, 21, 24, 25) sts]

9 • Rep step 8 (last 2 rows) 2 (2, 3, 3, 3) more times. [12 (13, 15, 18, 19) sts]

10 • Work even in st patt as established until 18 (18½, 19, 19½, 20)" from beg. Fasten off.

Sleeve (Make 2)

1 • Ch 30 (32, 34, 34, 36).

FOUNDATION ROW (WS): Sc in 2nd ch from hk (count as st) and in each ch to end, turn. [29 (31, 33, 33, 35) sts]

2 • **ROW 2:** Ch 1, sc in first and each st to end, turn. **ROW 3:** Ch 1, sc in first 1 (2, 0, 0, 1) st, pm, sc in each st across to last 1 (2, 0, 0, 1) st, pm, sc in each st to end, turn.

3 • **ROW 4 (INC):** Ch 1, 2 sc in first st, sc in each st to marker, sc in each of next 3 sts, *FPDC around each of next 3 sc in row below, sc in each of next 3 sts*, rep from * to * to marker, sc in each st to last st, 2 sc in last st, turn. [31 (33, 35, 35, 37) sts]
Starting with row 5 of Repeating Cables st patt (see page 34) as established between markers, inc as foll:

4 • Work 3 rows even in st patt as established.
NEXT ROW (INC): Ch 1, 2 sc in first st, patt as established to last st, 2 sc in last st, turn. [33 (35, 37, 37, 39) sts]

5 • Rep step 4 (last 4 rows) 4 (4, 0, 6, 8) more times. [41 (43, 37, 49, 55) sts]

6 • Work 5 rows even in st patt as established.
NEXT ROW (INC): Ch 1, 2 sc in first st, patt as established to last st, 2 sc in last st, turn. [43 (45, 39, 51, 57) sts]

7 • Rep step 6 (last 6 rows) 7 (7, 10, 6, 5) more times. [57 (59, 59, 63, 67) sts]

8 • Work even in Repeating Cables st patt as established until 17½ (17½, 18, 18, 18½)", ending with WS row complete.

SLEEVE CAP

9 • **NEXT ROW (DEC; RS):** Ch 1, sc in first st, patt as established to last 3 sts, sc in next st, turn. Rem sts unworked. [55 (57, 57, 61, 65) sts]

10 • **NEXT ROW (DEC):** Ch 1, sc in first st, patt as established to last 3 sts, sc in last st, turn. Rem sts unworked. [53 (55, 55, 59, 63) sts]

11 • **NEXT ROW (DEC):** Ch 1, sc2tog, sc in next st, patt as established to last 2 sts, sc2tog, turn. [51 (53, 53, 57, 61) sts]

NEXT ROW: Ch 1, sc in first st, patt as established to last st, sc in last st, turn.

12 • Rep step 11 (last 2 rows) 6 more times. [39 (41, 41, 45, 49) sts]
Fasten off.

Neckband

1 • Sew back to front at right shoulder.

2 • Pm on back at inner edge of left shoulder 3½ (3¾, 4¼, 5¼, 5½)" from corner. Join yarn with sc (count as st) at inner corner of shoulder on left front neck. With RS facing, work evenly spaced sts as foll:
ROW 1 (RS): LEFT FRONT: 9 (9, 11, 11, 13) sc;
FRONT NECK BASE: 9 (11, 9, 11, 11) sc;
RIGHT FRONT: 10 (10, 12, 12, 14) sc;
BACK: 18 (20, 22, 24, 24) sc to marker, turn. [47 (51, 55, 59, 63) sts]
Remove marker.

3 • **ROW 2:** Ch 1, sc in first 1 (0, 2, 1, 0) st, pm, sc in each st to last 1 (0, 2, 1, 0) st, pm, sc in each st to end, turn.

4 • **ROW 3:** Ch 1, sc in first and each st to marker, sc in each of next 3 sts, *FPDC around each of next 3 sc in row below, sc in each of next 3 sts*, rep from * to * to marker, sc in each st to end, turn.

5 • Cont even in Repeating Cables st patt as established between markers (starting with row 5, see page 34), until neckband measures 3" from beg. Fasten off.

Finishing

1 • With RS tog, sew back to front at left shoulder and neckband.

2 • Sew sleeves into body, centering the top of each sleeve on a shoulder seam. (See "Inserting Sleeves" on page 93.)

3 • Sew back to front at sides and underarms.

Bonnie Highlander

Delicate spirals and bold posts converge and split as you work your way up the body pieces of this comfortable tunic. Fellow stitchers are bound to admire the intriguing effect as the cable is hidden and revealed again. There are only two stitch patterns. One is used for the border, collar, sleeves, and yoke, and the other appears in the lower body.

YARN
Encore Worsted Weight from Plymouth, color #1607 Raspberry

Extra Small • 11 balls
Small • 12 balls
Medium • 12 balls
Large • 13 balls
Extra Large • 14 balls

SUPPLIES
7 (4.5 mm) crochet hook
H/8 (5 mm) crochet hook
4 stitch markers

GAUGE
16 sts and 18 rows to 4" in Twists and Posts st patt with H/8 (5 mm) hook
16 sts and 18 rows to 4" in Stretched Cables st patt with H/8 (5 mm) hook

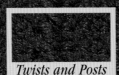
Twists and Posts

Stretched Cables

STRETCHED CABLES STITCH PATTERN

EXTRA SMALL, MEDIUM, AND EXTRA LARGE: Multiple of 12 sts + 3 sts (also add 1 ch for base ch)

SMALL AND LARGE: Multiple of 12 sts + 9 sts (also add 1 ch for base ch)

FOUNDATION ROW (RS): Sc in 2nd ch from hk (count as st) and in each ch to end, turn.

ROW 2: Ch 1, sc in each st to end, turn.

ROW 3: Ch 1, sc in each of first 3 sts, *FPDC around each of next 3 sc in row below (second, third, and fourth sts from edge or st marker), sc in each of next 3 sts*, rep from * to * to end, turn.

ROW 4: Ch 1, sc in first st and each st to end, turn.

Extra Small, Medium, and Extra Large Only

ROW 5: Ch 1, sc in each of first 3 sts, *cb3, sc in each of next 3 sts, FPDC around each of next 3 FPDC, sc in each of next 3 sts*, rep from * to * to end, turn.

Small and Large Only

ROW 5: Ch 1, sc in each of first 3 sts, *cb3, sc in each of next 3 sts, FPDC around each of next 3 FPDC, sc in each of next 3 sts*, rep from * to * to last 6 sts, cb3, sc in each st to end, turn.

All Sizes

ROW 6: Ch 1, sc in first st and each st to end, turn.

ROW 7: Ch 1, sc in each of first 3 sts, *FPDC around each of next 3 sts, sc in each of next 3 sts*, rep from * to * to end, turn.

ROWS 8–15: Rep rows 4–7 two more times.

ROWS 16 AND 18: Ch 1, sc in first st and each st to end, turn.

ROW 17: Ch 1, sc in each of first 3 sts, *cb3, sc in each of next 3 sts*, rep from * to * to end, turn.

ROW 19: Ch 1, sc in each of first 3 sts, *FPDC around each of next 3 sts, sc in each of next 3 sts*, rep from * to * to end, turn.

ROWS 20 AND 22: Ch 1, sc in first st and each st to end, turn.

Extra Small, Medium, and Extra Large Only

ROW 21: Ch 1, sc in each of first 3 sts, *FPDC around

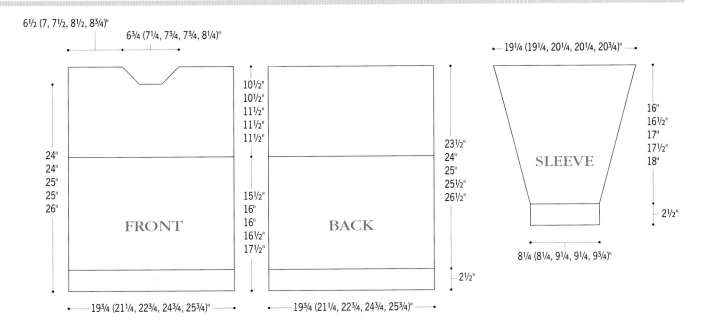

SIZING	Extra Small	Small	Medium	Large	Extra Large
To fit bust	31½"	34¼"	37¼"	41"	43¼"
Finished bust	39½"	42½"	45½"	49½"	51½"
Shoulder width	6½"	7"	7½"	8½"	8¾"
Sleeve length	18½"	19"	19½"	20"	20½"
Center back length	26"	26½"	27½"	28"	29"

each of next 3 sts, sc in each of next 3 sts, cb3, sc in each of next 3 sts*, rep from * to * to end, turn.

Small and Large Only

Row 21: Ch 1, sc in each of first 3 sts, *FPDC around each of next 3 sts, sc in each of next 3 sts, cb3, sc in each of next 3 sts*, rep from * to * to last 6 sts, FPDC around each of next 3 sts, sc in each st to end, turn.

All Sizes

Row 23: Ch 1, sc in each of first 3 sts, *FPDC around each of next 3 sts, sc in each of next 3 sts*, rep from * to * to end, turn.

Rows 24–31: Rep rows 20–23 two more times.

Rows 32–35: Rep rows 16–19.

Rows 4–35 form Stretched Cables st patt rep.

▦ TWISTS AND POSTS STITCH PATTERN

Multiple of 6 sts + 5 sts (also add 1 ch for base ch)

FOUNDATION ROW (RS): Sc in 2nd ch from hk (count as st) and in each ch to end, turn.

Row 2: Ch 1, sc in each st to end, turn.

Row 3: Ch 1, sc in first st, FPDC around next sc in row below (second st from edge or st marker), *sc in next st, FPDC around next sc in row below (second

st from last FPDC)*, rep from * to * to last st, sc in last st, turn.

Row 4: Ch 1, sc in first st and each st to end, turn.

Row 5: Ch 1, sc in first st, cr3, sc in next st, *FPDC around next FPDC in row below, sc in next st, cr3, sc in next st*, rep from * to * to end, turn.

Rows 4–5 form Twists and Posts st patt rep.

Dec and inc rows may interfere with st patt rep. Work complete or partial reps as desired unless indicated otherwise, using 2 sc sts at beg and 2 sc sts at end of row.

After placing st markers in a row, in subsequent rows move markers to current row as encountered.

Back

1 • With smaller hk, ch 80 (86, 92, 100, 104).

FOUNDATION ROW (RS): Sc in 2nd ch from hk (count as st) and in each ch to end, turn. [79 (85, 91, 99, 103) sts]

BORDER

2 • **Row 2:** Ch 1, sc in each of first 1 (1, 1, 2, 1) sts, pm, sc in each st to last 1 (1, 1, 2, 1) st, pm, sc in each st to end, turn.

3 • **Row 3:** Ch 1, sc in first and each st to marker, sc in next st, FPDC around next sc in row below, *sc in next st, FPDC around next sc in row below*, rep from * to * to st before marker, sc in next st, sc in each st to end, turn.

4 • **Row 4:** Ch 1, sc in first and each st to end, turn.

Row 5: Ch 1, sc in first and each st to marker, sc in next st, cr3, sc in next st, *FPDC around next FPDC in row below, sc in next st, cr3, sc in next st*, rep from * to * to marker, sc in each st to end, turn.

5 • Rep step 4 (last 2 rows) until 2½" from beg, ending with WS row complete, turn. Remove markers.

PATTERN CHANGE

Change to larger hk.

6 • **Next Row (RS):** Ch 1, sc in each of first 2 (2, 2, 3, 2) sts, pm, sc in each of next 2 sts, *TWL, FPDC around next FPDC, TWR, sc in next st*, rep from * to * to last 3 (3, 3, 4, 3) sts, sc in next st, pm, sc in last 2 (2, 2, 3, 2) sts, turn.

7 • **Next Row:** Ch 1, sc in first and each st to end, turn.

8 • **Next Row:** Ch 1, sc in first and each st to marker, sc in each of next 3 sts, *FPDC around each of next 3 sts, sc in each of next 3 sts*, rep from * to * to marker, sc in each st to end, turn.

Note: Twists and Posts st patt and Stretched Cables st patt feature cables with similar names: cr3 and .cb3. Switch to correct 3-post st to work Stretched Cables st pat.

STRETCHED CABLES BODY

9 • Starting with row 4, work Stretched Cables st patt between markers, with sc border sts, until 15½ (16, 16, 16½, 17½)" from beg, ending with WS row complete. Remove markers.

TWISTS AND POSTS YOKE

10 • **Next Row (RS):** Ch 1, sc in each of first 1 (1, 1, 2, 1) st, pm, sc in next st, FPDC around next sc in row below, *sc in next st, TWR, FPDC around next FPDC in row below, TWL*, rep from * to * to last 4 (4, 4, 5, 4) sts, sc in next st, FPDC around next sc in row below, sc in next st, pm, sc in last 1 (1, 1, 2, 1) st, turn.

11 • **Next Row:** Ch 1, sc in first and each st to end, turn.

12 • **Next Row:** Ch 1, sc in first and each st to marker, sc in first st, cr3, sc in next st, *FPDC around next FPDC in row below, sc in next st, cr3, sc in next st*, rep from * to * to marker, sc in each st to end, turn.

13 • Starting with row 4, work even in Twists and Posts st patt until 26 (26½, 27½, 28, 29)" from beg. Fasten off.

Front

1 • Work as for back, steps 1–13, until 24 (24, 25, 25, 26)" from beg, ending with RS row complete.

RIGHT NECK SHAPING

2 • **Next Row (Dec; WS):** Patt as established across next 31 (33, 35, 39, 40) sts, sc in next st, sc2tog, turn. Rem sts unworked. [33 (35, 37, 41, 42) sts]

3 • **Next Row (Dec):** Ch 1, sc2tog, sc in next st, patt as established to end, turn. [32 (34, 36, 40, 41) sts]

4 • **Next Row (Dec):** Patt as established to last 3 sts, sc in next st, sc2tog, turn. [31 (33, 35, 39, 40) sts]

Next Row (Dec): Ch 1, sc2tog, sc in next st, patt as established to end, turn. [30 (32, 34, 38, 39) sts]

5 • Rep step 4 (last 2 rows) 2 more times. [26 (28, 30, 34, 35) sts]

6 • Work even in st patt as established until 26 (26½, 27½, 28, 29)" from beg. Fasten off.

LEFT NECK SHAPING

7 • With WS facing, working into last full-width row and starting at inner right front shoulder shaping, sk next 11 (13, 15, 15, 17) sts. Join yarn with sc2tog (count as st). Working in patt as previously established on last full-width row, cont as foll:

Next Row (WS): Sc in next st, patt as established to end, turn. [33 (35, 37, 41, 42) sts]

8 • **Next Row (Dec):** Patt as established to last 3 sc, sc in next st, sc2tog, turn. [32 (34, 36, 40, 41) sts]

9 • **Next Row (Dec):** Ch 1, sc2tog, sc in next st, patt as established to end, turn. [31 (33, 35, 39, 40) sts]

Next Row (Dec): Patt as established to last 3 sc, sc in next st, sc2tog, turn. [30 (32, 34, 38, 39) sts]

10 • Rep step 9 (last 2 rows) 2 more times. [26 (28, 30, 34, 35) sts]

11 • Work even in st patt as established until 26 (26½, 27½, 28, 29)" from beg. Fasten off.

Sleeve (Make 2)

1 • With smaller hk, ch 34 (34, 38, 38, 40).

Foundation Row (RS): Sc in 2nd ch from hk (count as st) and in each ch to end. [33 (33, 37, 37, 39) sts]

CUFF

2 • **Row 2 (WS):** Ch 1, sc in each of first 2 (2, 1, 1, 2) sts, pm, sc in each st to last 2 (2, 1, 1, 2) sts, pm, sc in each st to end, turn.

3 • **Row 3:** Ch 1, sc in first and each st to marker, sc in next st, FPDC around next sc in row below, *sc in next st, FPDC around next sc in row below*, rep from * to * to st before marker, sc in next st, sc in each st to end, turn.

4 • **Row 4:** Ch 1, sc in first and each st to end, turn.

5 • **Row 5:** Ch 1, sc in first and each st to marker, sc in first st, cr3, sc in next st, *FPDC around next FPDC in row below, sc in next st, cr3, sc in next st*, rep from * to * to marker, sc in each st to end, turn.

6 • Starting with row 4, work even in Twists and Posts st patt as established until 2½" from beg, ending with WS row complete, turn.

BODY

Change to larger hk. Working in st patt as established, cont as foll:

7 • **Next Row (Inc; RS):** Ch 1, 2 sc in first st, sc in each st to marker, patt as established to marker, sc in each st to last st, 2 sc in last st, turn. [35 (35, 39, 39, 41) sts]

Next Row: Ch 1, sc in first and each st to marker, patt as established to marker, sc in each st to end, turn.

8 • Rep step 7 (last 2 rows) 8 more times. [51 (51, 55, 55, 57) sts]

9 • **Next Row (Inc):** Ch 1, 2 sc in first st, sc in each st to marker, patt as established to marker, sc in each st to last st, 2 sc in last st, turn. [53 (53, 57, 57, 59) sts]

Cont even in st patt as established and maintaining sc borders at either sides of work for 3 more rows.

10 • Rep step 9 (last 4 rows) 12 more times. [77 (77, 81, 81, 83) sts]

11 • Work even in st patt as established until 18½ (19, 19½, 20, 20½)" from beg. Fasten off.

Neckband

1 • Sew back to front at right shoulder.

2 • Mark inner edge of left shoulder on back with marker 6½ (7, 7½, 8½, 8¾)" from corner.

3 • With smaller hk and RS facing, join yarn with sc (count as st) at marker on left front neck edge and work evenly spaced sts as foll:
Row 1 (RS): Left Front Slope: 8 (10, 10, 12, 13) sc;
Front Neck Base: 11 (13, 15, 15, 17) sc;
Right Front Slope: 9 (11, 11, 13, 14) sc;
Back Neck: 24 (24, 28, 30, 32) sc, turn. [53 (59, 65, 71, 77) sts]

4 • **Row 2:** Ch 1, sc in first and each st to end, turn.

5 • **Row 3:** Ch 1, sc in first st, FPDC around next sc in row below, *sc in next st, FPDC around next sc in row below*, rep from * to * to last st, sc in last st, turn.

6 • **Row 4:** Ch 1, sc in first and each st to end, turn.

7 • **Row 5:** Ch 1, sc in first st, cr3, sc in next st, *FPDC around next FPDC in row below, sc in next st, cr3, sc in next st*, rep from * to * to end, turn.

8 • Starting with row 4, cont in Twists and Posts st patt as established until 2½" from beg. Fasten off.

Finishing

1 • Sew back to front at left shoulder and collar.

2 • On front and back, pm at each side (vertical edge) 9½ (9½, 10, 10, 10¼)" below shoulder seam. Mark inside corner of left shoulder on back in same manner. Sew sleeves into body between markers. (See "Inserting Sleeves" on page 93.)

3 • Sew back to front at sides and underarms.

Slanted Posts

Pastel Heather

Like groups of heather in a garden, bands of soft color enhance this long, loose-fitting sweater. There are no crossed or twisted posts in this design, just basic stitches combined to create the illusion of cables running vertically up the sweater. Only one color and one stitch pattern is worked in each row. The body and sleeves are worked from side to side.

YARN

Decor from Patons in the following colors:
#1621 Country Blue (color A),
#1645 Pale Country Pink (color B),
#1625 Pale Aubergine (color C),
#1635 Pale Sage Green (color D),
#1720 Pale Taupe Heather (color E)

Extra Small	• 2 balls of each color
Small	• 2 balls of each color
Medium	• 3 balls of each color
Large	• 3 balls of each color
Extra Large	• 3 balls of each color

SUPPLIES

H/8 (5 mm) crochet hook
2 stitch markers

GAUGE

14 sts and 16 rows to 4" in
Slanted Posts st patt

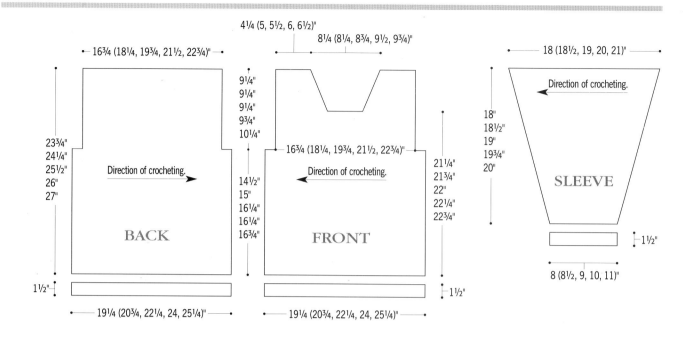

SIZING	Extra Small	Small	Medium	Large	Extra Large
To fit bust	31½"	34¼"	37¼"	41"	43¼"
Finished bust	38½"	41½"	44½"	48"	50½"
Shoulder width	4¼"	5"	5½"	6"	6½"
Sleeve length	19½"	20"	20½"	21¼"	21½"
Center back length	25¼"	25¾"	27"	27½"	28½"

SLANTED POSTS STITCH PATTERN

Multiple of 2 sts + 5 sts (also add 1 ch for base ch)

FOUNDATION ROW (RS): Sc in 2nd ch from hk (count as st) and in each ch to end, turn.

Row 2: Ch 1, sc in each st to end, turn.

Row 3: Ch 1, sc in each of first 3 sts, *ch 1, sk next st, sc in next st*, rep from * to * to end, turn.

Row 4: Ch 1, sc in each st and ch-sp to end, turn.

Row 5: Ch 1, [insert hk in first st in previous row, YO, draw through lp, tr in first sk st in row below, YO, draw through rem 2 lps on hk, do not sk st in previous row (sctr2tog made)], sc in next st, *tr in next sk st in row below, sk st behind tr just made, sc in next st*, rep from * to * to last 3 sts, sc in each st to end, turn.

ROWS 6 AND 7: Ch 1, sc in each st to end, turn.

Rows 2–7 form Slanted Posts st patt rep.

Back

Work sideways from left side to right side.

LEFT ARMHOLE SHAPING

1 • With A, ch 52 (54, 58, 58, 60).

FOUNDATION ROW (RS): Sc in 2nd ch from hk (count as st) and in each ch to end, turn. [51 (53, 57, 57, 59) sc]

2 • Work rows 2–5 of Slanted Posts st patt. (See first column on this page.)

BODY

3 • ROW 6 (INC; WS): Ch 33 (33, 33, 35, 37), sc in 2nd ch from hk (count as st) and each of next 31 (31, 31, 33, 35) ch, sc in next and each st to end, turn. [83 (85, 89, 91, 95) sc]

4 • ROW 7: Ch 1, sc in each st to end, turn.

5 • ROW 8 (MOCK CABLE): With E, ch 1, sc in first st, *hdc in next st, sl st loosely in next st*, rep from * to * to last 2 sts, hdc in next st, sc in last st, turn.

6 • ROW 9: With B, ch 1, sc in each st to end, turn.

Work rows 2–7 of Slanted Posts st patt.

7 • Work step 5 (row 8) once more.

8 • Work even, alternating Slanted Posts st patt with Mock Cable row and changing colors each rep, cont as foll:

Rep step 6 with C, then step 5 with E.

Rep step 6 with D, then step 5 with E.

Rep step 6 with A, then step 5 with E.

Rep step 6 with B, then step 5 with E.

9 • Rep step 8 until 18 (19½, 21, 22¾, 24)" from beg, ending with WS row complete.

Note: Length from beg is width of garment.

RIGHT ARMHOLE SHAPING

10 • NEXT ROW (DEC; RS): Patt as established over next 51 (53, 57, 57, 59) sts, turn. Rem 32 (32, 32, 34, 36) sts unworked.

11 • Cont even in st patts and color sequence as established until 19¼ (20¾, 22¼, 24, 25¼)". Fasten off.

Front

Work sideways from right side to left side.

1 • Starting with step 1, work as for back until 5½ (6¼, 6¾, 7¼, 7¾)" from beg, ending with WS row complete.

RIGHT NECK SHAPING

Working in color sequence and alternating Slanted Posts st patt and Mock Cable row as established, cont as foll:

2 • NEXT ROW (DEC; RS): Patt as established across first 78 (80, 82, 82, 84) sts, sc in next st, sc2tog, turn. Rem sts unworked. [80 (82, 84, 84, 86) sts]

3 • NEXT ROW (DEC): Ch 1, sc2tog, sc in next st, patt as established to end, turn. [79 (81, 83, 83, 85) sts]

NEXT ROW (DEC): Patt as established to last 3 sts, sc in next st, sc2tog, turn. [78 (80, 82, 82, 84) sts]

4 • Rep step 3 (last 2 rows) 2 more times. [74 (76, 78, 78, 80) sts]

5 • Work even in color sequence and alternating Slanted Posts st patt and Mock Cable row as established until 12 (12¾, 13¾, 15, 15¾)" from beg, ending with WS row complete.

LEFT NECK SHAPING

6 • NEXT ROW (INC; RS): Patt as established to last 2 sts, sc in next st, 2 sc in next st, turn. [75 (77, 79, 79, 81) sts]

7 • NEXT ROW (INC): Ch 1, 2 sc in first st, sc in next st, patt as established to end, turn. [76 (78, 80, 80, 82) sts]

NEXT ROW (INC): Patt as established to last 2 sts, sc in next st, 2 sc in last st, turn. [77 (79, 81, 81, 83) sts]

8 • Rep step 7 (last 2 rows) 2 more times. [81 (83, 85, 85, 87) sts]

9 • NEXT ROW (INC): Ch 3 (3, 5, 7, 9), sc in 2nd ch from hk (count as st) and each rem ch, patt as established to end, turn. [83 (85, 89, 91, 95) sts]

10 • Cont patt as established until 18 (19½, 21, 22¾, 24)" from beg, ending with WS row complete.

LEFT ARMHOLE SHAPING

11 • Work as for back, steps 10 and 11, right armhole shaping.

Sleeve (Make 2)

Work from underarm to underarm.

1 • With A, ch 4 (6, 8, 10, 12).

FOUNDATION ROW (INC; RS): Sc in 2nd ch from hk (count as st) and in each ch to last ch, 2 sc in last ch, turn. [4 (6, 8, 10, 12) sts]

2 • ROW 2 (INC): Ch 6, sc in 2nd ch from hk (count as st) and each of next 4 ch, sc in next and each st to end, turn. [9 (11, 13, 15, 17) sts]

3 • ROW 3 (INC): Ch 1, sc in each of first 3 sts, *ch 1, sk next st, sc in next st*, rep from * to * to last 2 sts, ch 1, sk next st, 2 sc in last st, turn. [10 (12, 14, 16, 18) sts]

4 • ROW 4 (INC): Ch 6, sc in 2nd ch from hk (count as st), and each of next 4 ch, sc in next st, pm, sc in next and each st and ch-sp to end, turn. [15 (17, 19, 21, 23) sts]

5 • ROW 5 (INC): Ch 1, sctr2tog, *tr in next sk st in row below, sk st behind tr just made, sc in next st*, rep from * to * to last 3 sts before marker, sc in next 3 sts, remove marker, sc in each st to last st, 2 sc in last st, turn. [16 (18, 20, 22, 24) sts]

6 • ROW 6 (INC): Ch 6, sc in 2nd ch from hk (count as st), and each of next 4 ch, sc in each st to end, turn. [21 (23, 25, 27, 29) sts]

7 • ROW 7 (INC): Ch 1, sc in each st to last st, 2 sc in last st, turn. [22 (24, 26, 28, 30) sts]

8 • ROW 8 (INC): With E, ch 6, sc in 2nd ch from hk (count as st), and each of next 4 ch, sc in each of next 2 sts, *hdc in next st, sl st loosely in next st*, rep from * to * to last 2 sts, hdc in next st, sc in last st, turn. [27 (29, 31, 33, 35) sts]

9 • ROW 9 (INC): With B, ch 1, sc in first and each st to last st, 2 sc in last st, turn. [28 (30, 32, 34, 36) sts]

10 • Rep steps 2–8 (rows 2–8). [51 (53, 55, 57, 59) sts]

11 • With C, as step 9 (row 9). [52 (54, 56, 58, 60) sts]

12 • Rep steps 2–4 (rows 2–4). [63 (65, 67, 69, 71) sts]

13 • NEXT ROW: Ch 1, sctr2tog, *tr in next sk st in row below, sk st behind tr just made, sc in next st*, rep from * to * to 3 sts before marker, sc in next 3 sts, remove marker, sc in each st to end, turn.

14 • Cont even in color sequence, alternating Slanted Posts st patt and Mock Cable row until 13 (13 1/2, 14, 15, 16)" from beg, ending with WS row complete.

15 • NEXT ROW (DEC; RS): Patt as established to last 7 sts, sc in next st, sc2tog, turn. Rem sts unworked. [58 (60, 62, 64, 66) sts]

NEXT ROW (DEC): Ch 1, sc2tog, patt as established to end, turn. [57 (59, 61, 63, 65) sts]

16 • Rep step 15 (last 2 rows) 9 more times. [3 (5, 7, 9, 11) sts]
Fasten off.

Back Border

1 • With RS of back facing, join E with sc (count as st) in first row end and work evenly spaced sts into row ends along bottom edge as foll:

2 • ROW 1 (RS): 56 (60, 66, 70, 74) sc to opposite side. Fasten off. Turn work. [57 (61, 67, 71, 75) sts]

3 • ROW 2: With D, join yarn with sc in last st of previous row, *hdc in next st, sl st loosely in next st*, rep from * to * to last 2 sts, hdc in next st, sc in last st. Fasten off. Don't turn.

4 • Rep step 3 (last row) 4 more times, changing color each row in foll sequence: C, B, A, E.

Front Border

Work as for back border.

Cuff (Make 2)

1 • With RS facing, join E with sc (count as st) at first row end of sleeve bottom, and work evenly spaced sts as foll:

ROW 1 (RS): 30 (32, 34, 38, 42) sc to opposite side. Fasten off. Turn work. [31 (33, 35, 39, 43) sts]

2 • Work as for back border, steps 3 and 4.

Neckband

Note: Work all sts loosely.

1 • Sew back to front at right shoulder seam.

2 • Mark inner edge of left shoulder on back with marker 4¼ (5, 5½, 6, 6½)" from corner.

3 • With RS facing, join E with sc (count as st) at left front neck edge (inner corner of shoulder), and work evenly spaced sts in row ends as foll:
ROW 1 (RS): LEFT FRONT SLOPE: 6 (8, 8, 10, 10) sc;
FRONT NECK BASE: 16 (18, 18, 20, 20) sc;
RIGHT FRONT NECK SLOPE: 7 (9, 9, 11, 11) sc;
BACK NECK: 25 (25, 27, 27, 29) sc to marker. Fasten off. Turn work. [55 (61, 63, 69, 71) sts]

4 • Work as for back border, steps 2 and 3.

5 • With RS tog, sew back to front at left shoulder and neckband.

Finishing

1 • Sew sleeves into body, centering the top of each sleeve on a shoulder seam. (See "Inserting Sleeves" on page 93.)

2 • Sew back to front at sides and underarms.

Double Spiral

From its stitches and shaping through to the silhouette, this sweater is meant to enhance your figure. Like the vintage sweaters that inspired this creation, a semi-fitted upper body gives way to a subtle flared hem. The shaping implies womanly curves while the well-defined vertical cables create a slimming effect. The sleeves repeat the shaping by flaring out at the cuff and ending with a feminine scallop edging. A beginning crocheter can easily stitch this garment.

YARN

Super 10 from Butterfly, color #3945 Purple

Extra Small	•	7 balls
Small	•	8 balls
Medium	•	8 balls
Large	•	9 balls
Extra Large	•	10 balls

SUPPLIES

H/8 (5 mm) crochet hook
2 stitch markers

GAUGE

16 sts and 17 rows to 4" in Corkscrew Cable st patt

Corkscrew Cable

Flared Corkscrew Cable

FLARED CORKSCREW CABLE STITCH PATTERN

Multiple of 6 sts + 7 sts (also add 1 ch for base ch)

FOUNDATION ROW (WS): Sc in 2nd ch from hk (count as st) and in each ch to end, turn.

Row 2: Ch 1, sc in first 3 sts, *ch 1, sk next st, sc in each of next 5 sts*, rep from * to * to last 4 sts, ch 1, sk next st, sc in each of next 3 sts, turn.

Row 3: Ch 1, sc in first and each st and ch-sp to end, turn.

Row 4: Ch 1, sc in each of first 2 sts, *working in front of fabric, make 3 dc in sk st in row below, sk 3 sc behind 3 dc just made, sc in each of next 3 sts*, rep from * to * to last 5 sts, 3 dc in next sk st in row below, sk 3 sc behind 3 dc just made, sc in each of last 2 sts, turn.

Row 5: Ch 1, sc in first and each st to end, turn.

Row 6: Ch 1, sc in each of first 2 sts, *cb3, sc in each of next 3 sts*, rep from * to * to last 5 sts, cb3, sc in each of last 2 sts, turn.

Rows 5–6 form Flared Corkscrew Cable st patt rep.

CORKSCREW CABLE STITCH PATTERN

Multiple of 5 sts + 5 sts (also add 1 ch for base ch)

FOUNDATION ROW (WS): Sc in 2nd ch from hk (count as st) and in each ch to end, turn.

Row 2: Ch 1, sc in first 2 sts, *ch 1, sk next st, sc in each of next 4 sts*, rep from * to * to last 3 sts, ch 1, sk next st, sc in each of last 2 sts, turn.

Row 3: Ch 1, sc in first and each st and ch-sp to end, turn.

Row 4: Ch 1, sc in first st, *working in front of fabric make 3 dc in sk st in row below, sk 3 sc behind 3 dc just made, sc in each of next 2 sts*, rep from * to * to last 4 sts, 3 dc in next sk st in row below, sk 3 sc behind 3 dc just made, sc in last st, turn.

Row 5: Ch 1, sc in first and each st to end, turn.

Row 6: Ch 1, sc in first st, *cb3, sc in each of next 2 sts*, rep from * to * to last 4 sts, cb3, sc in last st, turn.

Rows 5–6 form Corkscrew Cable st patt rep.

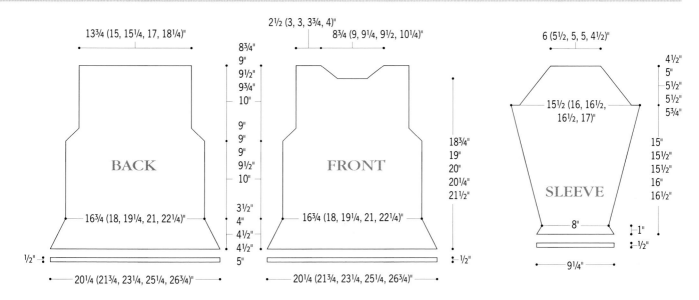

SIZING	Extra Small	Small	Medium	Large	Extra Large
To fit bust	31½"	34¼"	37¼"	41"	43¼"
Finished bust	33½"	36"	38½"	42"	44½"
Shoulder width	2½"	3"	3"	3¾"	4"
Sleeve length	20"	21"	21½"	22"	22¾"
Center back length	21¾"	22½"	23½"	24¼"	25½"

Back

1 • Ch 82 (88, 94, 102, 108).

FOUNDATION ROW (WS): Sc in 2nd ch from hk (count as st) and in each ch to end, turn. [81 (87, 93, 101, 107) sts]

FLARED HEM

2 • ROW 2 (RS): Ch 1, sc in each of first 1 (1, 1, 2, 2) st, pm, sc in next 3 sts, *ch 1, sk next st, sc in each of next 5 sts*, rep from * to * to last 5 (5, 5, 6, 6) sts, ch 1, sk next st, sc in each of next 3 sts, pm, sc in each st to end, turn.

3 • ROW 3: Ch 1, sc in first and each st and ch-sp to end, turn.

4 • ROW 4: Ch 1, sc in each st to marker, sc in each of next 2 sts, *3 dc in sk st in row below, sk 3 sc behind dc just made, sc in each of next 3 sts*, rep from * to * to 5 sts before marker, 3 dc in next sk st in row below, sk 3 sc behind 3 dc just made, sc in each of next 2 sts, sc in each st to end, turn.

5 • Starting with row 5, work Flared Corkscrew Cable st patt (see previous page) as established until 3½ (4, 4½, 4½, 5)" from beg, ending with WS row complete.

BODY

6 • NEXT ROW (DEC; RS): Ch 1, sc in first and each st to marker, sc2tog, *cb3, sc in next st, sc2tog*, rep from * to * to 5 sts before marker, cb3, sc2tog, sc in each st to end, turn. [67 (72, 77, 84, 89) sts]

7 • NEXT ROW: Ch 1, sc in first and each st to end, turn.

8 • NEXT ROW: Ch 1, sc in each st to marker, sc in next st, *cb3, sc in each of next 2 sts*, rep from * to * to last 4 sts before marker, cb3, sc in next st, sc in each st to end, turn.

9 • Starting with row 5, work Corkscrew Cable st patt (see previous page) as established until 12½ (13, 13½, 14, 15)" from beg, ending with WS row complete.

ARMHOLE SHAPING

10 • NEXT ROW (DEC; RS): Patt as established to last st, turn. Rem st unworked. [66 (71, 76, 83, 88) sts]

11 • NEXT ROW (DEC): Ch 1, sc2tog, patt as established to last 3 sts, sc2tog, turn. Rem st unworked. [63 (68, 73, 80, 85) sts]

12 • NEXT ROW (DEC): Ch 1, sc2tog, patt as established to last 2 sts, sc2tog, turn. [61 (66, 71, 78, 83) sts]

13 • Rep step 12 (last row) 3 (3, 5, 5, 5) more times. [55 (60, 61, 68, 73) sts]

14 • Cont even in st patt as established until 21¼ (22, 23, 23¾, 25)" from beg. Fasten off.

Front

1 • Work as for back, steps 1–14, until 18¾ (19, 20, 20¼, 21½)" from beg, ending with WS row complete.

LEFT NECK SHAPING

2 • NEXT ROW (DEC; RS): Patt as established across first 19 (21, 21, 24, 25) sts, sc2tog, turn. Rem sts unworked. [20 (22, 22, 25, 26) sts]

3 • NEXT ROW (DEC): Ch 1, sc2tog, patt as established to end, turn. [19 (21, 21, 24, 25) sts]

NEXT ROW (DEC): Patt as established to last 2 sts, sc2tog, turn. [18 (20, 20, 23, 24) sts]

4 • Rep step 3 (last 2 rows) 4 more times. [10 (12, 12, 15, 16) sts]

5 • Work even in Corkscrew Cable st patt as established until 21¼ (22, 23, 23¾, 25)" from beg. Fasten off.

RIGHT NECK SHAPING

6 • With RS facing, working into last full-width row and starting at inner left front shoulder shaping, sk next 13 (14, 15, 16, 19) sts. Join yarn with sc2tog (count as st) and work in st patt as established on last full-width row as foll:

NEXT ROW (RS): Patt as established to end, turn. [20 (22, 22, 25, 26) sts]

7 • NEXT ROW (DEC): Patt as established to last 2 sc, sc2tog, turn. [19 (21, 21, 24, 25) sts]

NEXT ROW (DEC): Ch 1, sc2tog, patt as established to end, turn. [18 (20, 20, 23, 24) sts]

8 • Rep step 7 (last 2 rows) 4 more times. [10 (12, 12, 15, 16) sts]

9 • Work even in st patt as established until 21¼ (22, 23, 23¾, 25)" from beg. Fasten off.

Sleeve (Make 2)

1 • Ch 38.

FOUNDATION ROW (WS): Sc in 2nd ch from hk (count as st) and in each ch to end, turn. [37 sts]

FLARED HEM

2 • ROW 2 (RS): Ch 1, sc in each of first 3 sts, *ch 1, sk next st, sc in each of next 5 sts*, rep from * to * to last 4 sts, ch 1, sk next st, sc in each of last 3 sts, turn.

3 • ROW 3: Ch 1, sc in first and each st and ch-sp to end, turn.

4 • ROW 4: Ch 1, sc in each of first 2 sts, *3 dc in sk st in row below, sk 3 sc behind dc just made, sc in each of next 3 sts*, rep from * to * to end, turn.

5 • ROW 5: Ch 1, sc in first and each st to end, turn.

BODY

6 • ROW 6 (DEC; RS): Ch 1, sc in each of first 2 sts, *cb3, sc in next st, sc2tog*, rep from * to * to last 5 sts, cb3, sc in each of last 2 sts, turn. [32 sts]

7 • ROW 7: Ch 1, sc in first st, pm, sc in each st to last st, pm, sc in last st, turn.

8 • ROW 8: Ch 1, sc in each st to marker, sc in next st, *cb3, sc in each of next 2 sts*, rep from * to * to 5 sts before marker, cb3, sc in next st, sc in last st, turn.

Starting with row 5, work Corkscrew Cable st patt (see page 48) as established, working inc as foll:

9 • NEXT ROW: Ch 1, sc in first and each st to marker, patt as established to next marker, sc in each st to end, turn.

NEXT ROW (INC): Ch 1, 2 sc in first st, sc in each st to marker, patt to next marker, sc in each st to last st, 2 sc in last st, turn. [34 sts]

10 • Rep step 9 (last 2 rows) 2 (3, 4, 4, 5) more times. [38 (40, 42, 42, 44) sts]

11 • Work even 3 rows in st patt as established.

NEXT ROW (INC): Ch 1, 2 sc in first st, sc in each st to marker, patt to next marker, sc in each st to last st, 2 sc in last st, turn. [40 (42, 44, 44, 46) sts]

12 • Rep step 11 (last 4 rows) 11 more times. [62 (64, 66, 66, 68) sts]

13 • Work even in st patt until 15 (15½, 15½, 16, 16½)" from beg. End with WS row complete.

SLEEVE CAP

14 • NEXT ROW (DEC; RS): Patt as established to last st, turn. Rem st unworked. [61 (63, 65, 65, 67) sts]

15 • NEXT ROW (DEC): Ch 1, sc2tog, patt as established to last 3 sts, sc2tog, turn. Rem st unworked. [58 (60, 62, 62, 64) sts]

16 • NEXT ROW (DEC): Ch 1, sc2tog, patt as established to last 2 sts, sc2tog, turn. [56 (58, 60, 60, 62) sts]

17 • Rep step 16 (last row) 16 (18, 20, 20, 22) more times. [24 (22, 20, 20, 18) sts]
Fasten off.

Back Scallop Border

1 • With RS of back facing, join yarn with sc (count as st) in corner, work in lps of beg ch as foll:

2 • FOUNDATION ROW (RS): Sc in each of next 1 (1, 1, 2, 2) ch, *sk next 2 ch, 5 dc in next ch, sk next 2 ch, sc in next ch*, rep from * to * to last 1 (1, 1, 2, 2) ch, sc in each ch to end. [13 (14, 15, 16, 17) dc shells]
Fasten off.

Front Scallop Border

Work as for back scallop border.

Sleeve Scallop Border

1 • With RS facing, join yarn with sc (count as st) in corner of wrist, work in lps of beg ch as foll:

2 • FOUNDATION ROW (RS): *Sk next 2 ch, 5 dc in next ch, sk next 2 ch, sc in next ch*, rep from * to * to end.
Fasten off.

Neckband

1 • Sew back to front at right shoulder.

2 • Mark inner edge of left shoulder on back with marker.

3 • With RS facing, join yarn with sc (count as st) at inner corner of shoulder on front neck and work evenly spaced sts in edge as foll:

ROW 1 (RS): LEFT FRONT SLOPE: 9 (11, 11, 13, 13) sc;
FRONT NECK BASE: 13 (14, 15, 16, 19) sc;
RIGHT FRONT SLOPE: 10 (12, 12, 14, 14) sc;
BACK NECK: 28 (29, 30, 31, 32) sc to marker. [61 (67, 69, 75, 79) sts]
Do not turn.
Fasten off.

4 • ROW 2 (RS): Join yarn with sc in first st, sc in each of next 0 (0, 1, 1, 0) sts, *sk next 2 sts, 5 dc in next st, sk next 2 sts, sc in next st*, rep from * to * to last 0 (0, 1, 1, 0) sts, sc in each st to end. Fasten off.

5 • With RS tog, join back to front at left shoulder and collar.

Finishing

1 • Sew sleeves into body, centering the top of each sleeve on a shoulder seam. (See "Inserting Sleeves" on page 93.)

2 • Sew back to front at sides and underarms.

Bob and Weave

Take the path less traveled by making a pullover that showcases your stitching skills. This beauty has a more advanced pattern, so the design is best tackled when you are confident with crossing posts. In any given row, several stitches create woven cables that scroll around columns of bobbles. The main portions of the body and sleeves are worked in repeats of a single stitch pattern.

YARN

Decor from Patons, color #1645 Pale Country Pink

Extra Small • 8 balls
Small • 8 balls
Medium • 9 balls
Large • 9 balls
Extra Large • 10 balls

SUPPLIES

7 (4.5 mm) crochet hook
H/8 (5 mm) crochet hook
2 stitch markers

GAUGE

14 sts and 16 rows to 4" in Bob and Weave st patt with H/8 (5 mm) crochet hook

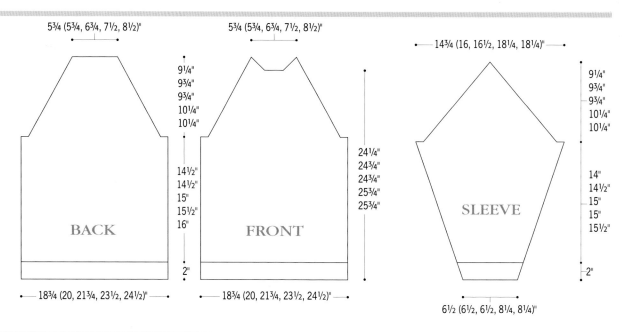

SIZING	Extra Small	Small	Medium	Large	Extra Large
To fit bust	31½"	34¼"	37¼"	41"	43¼"
Finished bust	37½"	40"	43½"	47"	49"
Shoulder and sleeve length	25¼"	26¼"	26¾"	27¼"	27¾"
Center back length	25¾"	26¼"	26¾"	27¾"	28¼"

BOB AND WEAVE STITCH PATTERN

Multiple of 12 sts (also add 1 ch for base ch)

FOUNDATION ROW (RS): Sc in 2nd ch from hk (count as st) and in each ch to end, turn.

ROW 2: Ch 1, sc in first and each st to end, turn.

ROW 3: Ch 1, *sc in first st, FPDC around next sc in row below (second st from edge, or third st from last FPDC in rep), sc in next st, FPDC around next sc in row below (second st from last FPDC), sc in each of next 4 sts, FPDC around next sc in row below (fifth st from last FPDC), sc in next st, FPDC around next sc in row below (second st from last FPDC), sc in next st*, rep from * to * to end, turn.

ROWS 4, 6, 8, 10, 12, AND 14: Ch 1, sc in first and each st to end, turn.

ROW 5: Ch 1, *sc in first st, TWL twice, sc in each of next 2 sts, TWR twice, sc in next st*, rep from * to * to end, turn.

ROW 7: Ch 1, *sc in each of first 2 sts, TWL, cr2R, TWR, sc in each of next 2 sts*, rep from * to * to end, turn.

ROW 9: Ch 1, *sc in each of first 3 sts, cb2, sc in each of next 2 sts, cb2, sc in each of next 3 sts*, rep from * to * to end, turn.

ROW 11: Ch 1, *sc in each of first 2 sts, TWR, cr2R, TWL, sc in each of next 2 sts*, rep from * to * to end, turn.

ROW 13: Ch 1, *sc in first st, TWR twice, sc in each of next 2 sts, TWL twice, sc in next st*, rep from * to * to end, turn.

ROWS 15 AND 17: Ch 1, *sc in first st, FPDC around next FPDC in row below, sc in next st, FPDC around next FPDC in row below, sc in each of next 4 sts, FPDC around next FPDC in row below, sc in next st, FPDC around next FPDC in row below, sc in next st*, rep from * to * to end, turn.

ROW 16: Ch 1, *sc in each of first 5 sts, bobble in next st (see page 85), sc in each of next 6 sts*, rep from * to * to end, turn.

Rows 4–17 form Bob and Weave st patt rep.

Back

1 • With smaller hk, ch 67 (71, 77, 83, 87).

FOUNDATION ROW (RS): Sc in 2nd ch from hk (count as st) and in each ch to end, turn. [66 (70, 76, 82, 86)]

BOBBLE ROAD BORDER

Pm after first 1 (1, 0, 1, 1) st and before last 2 (2, 1, 2, 2) sts.

2 • ROW 2 (WS): Ch 1, sc in first and each st to marker, sc in next st, *hdc in next st, sl st in next st*, rep from * to * to 2 sts before marker, hdc in next st, sc in next st, sc in each st to end, turn.

3 • ROWS 3 AND 5: Ch 1, sc in first and each st to end, turn.

4 • ROW 4: Ch 1, sc in first and each st to marker, sc in next 3 sts, *bobble in next st, sc in each of next 3 sts*, rep from * to * to marker, sc in each st to end, turn.

5 • ROW 6: Ch 1, sc in first and each st to marker, sc in next st, *hdc in next st, sl st in next st*, rep from * to * to marker, sc in each st to end, turn.

6 • ROW 7: Ch 1, sc in first and each st to end, turn. Remove markers.

BODY

Change to larger hk.

7 • ROW 8 (WS): Ch 1, sc in each of first 3 (5, 2, 5, 1) sts, pm, sc in next and each st to last 3 (5, 2, 5, 1) sts, pm, sc in next and each st to end, turn.

8 • ROW 9: Ch 1, sc in first and each st to marker, *sc in first st, FPDC around next sc in row below, sc in next st, FPDC around next sc in row below, sc in each of next 4 sts, FPDC around next sc in row below, sc in next st, FPDC around next sc in row below, sc in next st*, rep from * to * to marker, sc in each st to end, turn.

9 • Starting with row 4 of Bob and Weave st patt (see previous page), cont in st patt as established, until 16½ (16½, 17, 17½, 18)" from beg of bottom border, ending with WS row complete.

ARMHOLE SHAPING

10 • NEXT ROW (DEC; RS): Patt as established to last 5 (5, 6, 6, 6) sts, sc in each of next 2 sts, turn. Rem sts unworked. [63 (67, 72, 78, 82) sts]

11 • NEXT ROW (DEC): Ch 1, sc2tog, sc in next st, patt as established to last 6 (6, 7, 7, 7) sts, sc in next st, sc2tog, turn. Rem sts unworked. [58 (62, 66, 72, 76) sts]

12 • NEXT ROW (DEC): Ch 1, sc2tog, sc in next st, patt as established to last 3 sts, sc in next st, sc2tog, turn. [56 (60, 64, 70, 74) sts]

13 • Rep step 12 (last row) 2 (4, 4, 6, 6) more times. [52 (52, 56, 58, 62) sts]

14 • NEXT ROW: Ch 1, sc in each of first 2 sts, patt as established to last 2 sts, sc in each of last 2 sts, turn.

NEXT ROW (DEC): Ch 1, sc2tog, sc in next st, patt as established to last 3 sts, sc in next st, sc2tog, turn. [50 (50, 54, 56, 60) sts]

15 • Rep step 14 (last 2 rows) 15 more times. Remove markers. Fasten off. [20 (20, 24, 26, 30) sts]

Front

1 • Work as for back, steps 1–14.

2 • Rep step 14 for 12 (12, 11, 11, 10) more times. [26 (26, 32, 34, 40) sts]

RIGHT SHOULDER SHAPING

Note: You need to work a partial patt rep for shoulder shaping. As available sts dwindle, cont to work any posts, cables, twists, or bobbles that fall within remaining patt sts. To determine your position within the st patt rep, track the number of sts that have been decreased at each edge from the last full patt rep, and then count in this number from each end of rep asterisk [*] on current shoulder row. Use st markers to track remaining patt st area. When only 3 sts remain for patt rep, work all as sc.

3 • NEXT ROW (DEC; WS): Ch 1, sc in each of first 2 sts, patt as established across next 4 (4, 7, 7, 10) sts, sc in next st, sc2tog, turn. Rem sts unworked. [8 (8, 11, 11, 14) sts]

4 • Next Row (Dec): Ch 1, sc2tog, sc in next st, patt as established to last 3 sts, sc in next st, sc2tog, turn. [6 (6, 9, 9, 12) sts]

Next Row (Dec): Ch 1, sc in each of first 3 sts, patt as established to last 3 sts, sc in next st, sc2tog, turn. [5 (5, 8, 8, 11) sts]

5 • Rep step 4 (last 2 rows) for 0 (0, 1, 1, 2) more times. Remove markers. [5 sts]

6 • Next Row (Dec): Ch 1, sc2tog, sc in next st, sc2tog, turn. [3 sts]

Next Row (Dec): Ch 1, sc in next st, sc2tog, turn. [2 sts]

Next Row (Dec): Ch 1, sc2tog. Fasten off.

LEFT SHOULDER SHAPING

7 • With WS facing, working in last full-width row and starting at inner right front shoulder, sk next 8 (8, 8, 10, 10) sts. Join yarn with sc2tog and cont as foll:

8 • Next Row (Dec; WS): Sc in next st, patt as established to last 3 sts, sc in each of last 3 sts, turn. [8 (8, 11, 11, 14) sts]

9 • Next Row (Dec): Ch 1, sc2tog, sc in next st, patt as established to last 3 sts, sc in next st, sc2tog, turn. [6 (6, 9, 9, 12) sts]

Next Row (Dec): Ch 1, sc2tog, sc in next st, patt as established to last 3 sts, sc in last 3 sts, turn. [5 (5, 8, 8, 11) sts]

10 • Rep step 9 (last 2 rows) for 0 (0, 1, 1, 2) more times. Remove markers. [5 sts]

11 • Work as for right shoulder shaping, step 6.

Sleeve (Make 2)

1 • With smaller hk, ch 24 (24, 24, 30, 30).

Foundation Row (RS): Sc in 2nd ch from hk (count as st) and each ch to end. [23 (23, 23, 29, 29) sts]

BOBBLE ROAD BORDER

2 • Row 2 (WS): Ch 1, sc in first 0 (0, 0, 1, 1) sts, pm, sc in next st, *hdc in next st, sl st in next st*, rep from * to * to last 2 (2, 2, 3, 3) sts, hdc in next st, sc in next st, pm, sc in each of last 0 (0, 0, 1, 1) sts, turn.

3 • Next 4 Rows: As back Bobble Road border steps 3–5 (rows 3–6, see page 55). Remove markers.

4 • Row 7: Ch 1, sc in each of first 3 (3, 3, 1, 1) sts, *2 sc in next st, sc in each of next 3 sts*, rep from * to * to end, turn. [28 (28, 28, 36, 36) sts]

BODY

Change to larger hk.

5 • Row 8 (WS): Ch 1, sc in each of first 2 (2, 2, 6, 6) sts, pm, sc in next and each st to last 2 (2, 2, 6, 6) sts, pm, sc in each st to end, turn.

6 • Row 9: Ch 1, sc in first and each st to marker, *sc in next st, FPDC around next sc in row below, sc in next st, FPDC around next sc in row below, sc in each of next 4 sts, FPDC around next sc in row below, sc in next st, FPDC around next sc in row below, sc in next st*, rep from * to * to marker, sc in each st to end, turn.

7 • Row 10: Ch 1, sc in first and each st to end, turn.

Starting with row 5 of Bob and Weave st patt (see page 54), cont st patt as established and shape as foll:

8 • Row 11 (Inc): Ch 1, 2 sc in next first st, sc in each st to marker, patt as established to marker, sc in each st to last st, 2 sc in last st, turn. [30 (30, 30, 38, 38) sts]

9 • Work even in st patt as established for 3 rows.

Next Row (Inc): As step 8. [32 (32, 32, 40, 40) sts]

10 • Cont in st patt as established, rep step 9 (last 4 rows) 10 (12, 13, 12, 12) more times. [52 (56, 58, 64, 64) sts]

11 • Work even in st patt as established until 16 (16½, 17, 17, 17½)" from beg of border, ending with WS row complete.

RAGLAN SHAPING

12 • Next Row (Dec; RS): Patt as established to last 5 (5, 6, 6, 6) sts, sc in each of next 2 sts, turn. Rem sts unworked. [49 (53, 54, 60, 60) sts]

13 • Next Row (Dec): Ch 1, sc2tog, sc in next st, patt as established to last 6 (6, 7, 7, 7) sts, sc in next st, sc2tog, turn. Rem sts unworked. [44 (48, 48, 54, 54) sts]

14 • NEXT ROW (DEC): Ch 1, sc2tog, sc in next st, patt as established to last 3 sts, sc in next st, sc2tog, turn. [42 (46, 46, 52, 52) sts]

15 • Rep step 14 (last row) 8 (10, 10, 14, 14) more times. [26 (26, 26, 24, 24) sts]

16 • NEXT ROW: Ch 1, sc in each of first 2 sts, patt as established to last 2 sts, sc in each of last 2 sts, turn.

NEXT ROW (DEC): Ch 1, sc2tog, sc in next st, patt as established to last 3 sts, sc in next st, sc2tog, turn. [24 (24, 24, 22, 22) sts]

17 • Rep step 16 (last 2 rows) 11 (11, 11, 10, 10) more times, removing markers when too few sts are available to work st patt and subsequent rows are all sc. [2 sts]

18 • NEXT ROW: Ch 1, sc in each of 2 sts, turn.

19 • NEXT ROW: Ch 1, sc2tog. Fasten off.

Body Armhole Edging

1 • FOUNDATION ROW (RS): With larger hk and RS of back facing, join yarn with sc (count as st) at beg of raglan armhole edge, sc 36 (38, 38, 40, 40) sts along 1 raglan armhole edge, turn.

2 • ROW 2: Ch 1, sc in each of first 1 (0, 0, 1, 1) st, pm, sc in next st, *hdc in next st, sl st in next st*, rep from * to * to last 3 (2, 2, 3, 3) sts, hdc in next st, sc in next st, pm, sc in each of last 1 (0, 0, 1, 1) st, turn.

3 • NEXT 4 ROWS: As Back Bobble Road border steps 3–5 (rows 3–6). Remove markers. Fasten off.

4 • Rep Bobble Road border on rem raglan armhole edges of back and front.

Finishing

1 • With larger hk and RS of sleeve facing, join yarn with sc (count as st) and work 36 (38, 38, 40, 40) sc evenly spaced across 1 raglan edge. Fasten off.

2 • Rep step 1 on rem raglan edges of sleeves.

3 • Place 1 sleeve's diagonal raglan edge along corresponding edge of front. With WS tog at neck, sew edges with rows matching. Continue seam by sewing rem portion of body's raglan edge to short, horizontal row at beg of sleeve shaping.

4 • Attach rem raglan sleeve edges in same manner.

5 • Sew back to front at sides and under-arms.

Neckband

1 • With smaller hk and RS facing, join yarn with sc (count as st) at top of left sleeve, work evenly spaced sts as foll:

ROW 1 (RS): TOP OF LEFT FRONT: 4 sc;
LEFT FRONT SLOPE: 6 (6, 8, 8, 10) sc;
FRONT NECK BASE: 8 (8, 8, 10, 10) sc;
RIGHT FRONT SLOPE: 6 (6, 8, 8, 10) sc;
TOP OF RIGHT FRONT: 4 sc;
RIGHT SLEEVE: 1 sc in top;
TOP OF RIGHT BACK: 4 sc;
BACK NECK: 19 (19, 23, 25, 29) sc;
TOP OF LEFT BACK: 4 sc;
LEFT SLEEVE: 1 sc, turn. [57 (57, 65, 69, 77) sts]

ROW 2: Ch 1, sc in first and each st to end, turn.

2 • ROW 3: Ch 1, sc in first st, pm, sc in next st, *hdc in next st, sl st in next st*, rep from * to * to last 3 sts, hdc in next st, sc in next st, pm, sc in last st, turn.

3 • Work as for back, Bobble Road border, steps 2–6 (see page 55).

4 • NEXT ROW: Sc in first st sc in next st, *hdc in next st, sl st in next st*, rep from * to * to last 2 sts before marker, hdc in next st, sc in next st, sc in last st. Remove markers. Fasten off.

5 • With RS tog, join neckband at left shoulder.

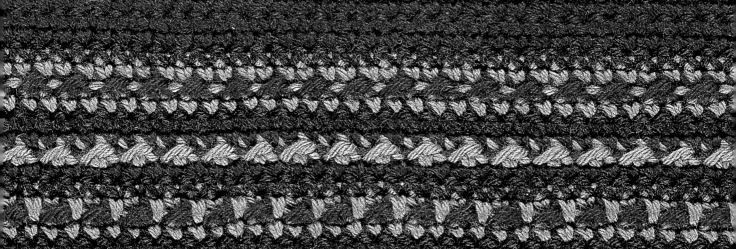

Twin Posts

Double Feature

Pairs of post stitches and a classic shape team up for a sweater that looks great in a wide range of sizes and colors. This is a crowd-pleaser. With unisex styling and sizing for chest measurements from 31½" to 48", you can make this garment for a woman, a teen boy or girl, or a man.

▌YARN

220 from Cascade, colors #7821 Beige, #4008 Cranberry, #9447 Forest Green, #9449 Navy

Yarn Color	Women's	Men's
A	Cranberry	Navy
B	Navy	Cranberry
C	Forest Green	Forest Green
D	Beige	Beige

Color A

Woman's Extra Small	• 7 balls
Woman's Small/ Man's Extra Small	• 8 balls
Woman's Medium/ Man's Small	• 8 balls
Woman's Large/ Man's Medium	• 9 balls
Woman's Extra Large/ Man's Large	• 9 balls
Woman's 2XL/ Man's Extra Large	• 10 balls
Woman's 3XL/ Man's 2XL	• 11 balls

Color B

All Sizes	• 1 ball

Color C

All Sizes	• 1 ball

Color D

All Sizes	• 1 ball

Supplies and gauge on the next page.

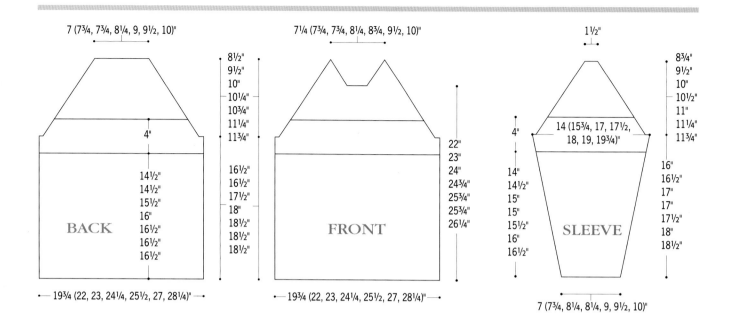

BACK

7 (7¾, 7¾, 8¼, 9, 9½, 10)"

8½"
9½"
10"
10¼"
10¾"
11¼"
11¾"

4"

14½"
14½"
15½"
16"
16½"
16½"
16½"

19¾ (22, 23, 24¼, 25½, 27, 28¼)"

FRONT

7¼ (7¾, 7¾, 8¼, 8¾, 9½, 10)"

22"
23"
24"
24¾"
25¾"
25¾"
26¼"

16½"
16½"
17½"
18"
18½"
18½"
18½"

19¾ (22, 23, 24¼, 25½, 27, 28¼)"

SLEEVE

1½"

8¾"
9½"
10"
10½"
11"
11¼"
11¾"

14 (15¾, 17, 17½, 18, 19, 19¾)"

4"

14"
14½"
15"
15"
15½"
16"
16½"

16"
16½"
17"
17"
17½"
18"
18½"

7 (7¾, 8¼, 8¼, 9, 9½, 10)"

SIZING

Women's Sizes	Extra Small	Small	Medium	Large	Extra Large	2XL	3XL
Men's Sizes		Extra Small	Small	Medium	Large	Extra Large	2XL
To fit bust/chest	31½"	34¼"	37¼"	41"	43¼"	46"	48"
Finished bust/chest	39½"	44"	46"	48½"	51"	54"	56½"
Shoulder/sleeve length	24¾"	26"	27"	27½"	28½"	29¼"	30¼"
Center back length	25"	26"	27½"	28¼"	29¼"	29¾"	30¼"

SUPPLIES

H/8 (5 mm) crochet hook
2 stitch markers

GAUGE

14 sts and 18 rows to 4" in
Twin Posts st patt

TWIN POSTS STITCH PATTERN

Multiple of 6 sts + 3 sts (also add 1 ch for base ch)

FOUNDATION ROW (WS): Sc in 2nd ch from hk (count as st) and in each ch to end, turn.

ROWS 2 AND 3: Ch 1, sc in first and each st to end, turn.

ROW 4: Ch 1, sc in each of first 3 sts, *FPDC around next sc in row below (fourth st from edge, or last FPDC), sc in next st, FPDC around next sc in row below (second st from last FPDC), sc in each of next 3 sts*, rep from * to * to end, turn.

ROW 5: Ch 1, sc in first and each st to end, turn.

ROW 6: Ch 1, sc in each of first 3 sts, *FPDC around next FPDC in row below, sc in next st, FPDC around next FPDC in row below, sc in each of next 3 sts*, rep from * to * to end, turn.

Rows 5–6 form Twin Posts st patt rep.

Back

1 • With A, ch 70 (78, 82, 86, 90, 96, 100).

FOUNDATION ROW (WS): Sc in 2nd ch from hk (count as st) and in each ch to end, turn. [69 (77, 81, 85, 89, 95, 99) sts]

2 • ROWS 2 AND 3: Ch 1, sc in first and each st to end, turn.

3 • ROW 4: Ch 1, sc in each of first 0 (1, 0, 2, 1, 1, 0) sts, pm, sc in each of next 3 sts, *FPDC around next sc in row below, sc in next st, FPDC around next sc in row below, sc in each of next 3 sts*, rep from * to * to last 0 (1, 0, 2, 1, 1, 0) sts, pm, sc in each st to end, turn.

4 • Starting with row 5, work even in Twin Posts st patt (see previous page) as established between markers until 14½ (14½, 15½, 16, 16½, 16½, 16½)" from beg, ending with RS row complete. Remove markers.

COLORED PEBBLES BAND

5 • Next Row (WS): Ch 1, sc in first and each st to end, turn.

6 • NEXT ROW: With B, ch 1, sc in first and each st to end, turn.

7 • NEXT ROW: With C, ch 1, sc in first and each st to end, turn.

8 • NEXT ROW: With D, ch 1, sc in first and each st to end, turn.

9 • NEXT ROW: With A, ch 1, sc in first st, *hdc in next st, sl st in next st*, rep from * to * to last 2 sts, hdc in next st, sc in last st, turn.

10 • NEXT ROW: With D, ch 1, sc in each of first 2 sts, *ssc in next st, sc in next st*, rep from * to * to last st, sc in last st, turn.

11 • NEXT ROW: With C, ch 1, sc in first and each st to end, turn.

12 • NEXT ROW: With B, ch 1, sc in first and each st to end, turn.

13 • NEXT ROW: With D, ch 1, sc in first st, *hdc in next st, sl st in next st*, rep from * to * to last 2 sts, hdc in next st, sc in last st, turn.

RAGLAN SHAPING

Rep Colored Pebbles band, steps 6–12, and AT THE SAME TIME shape work as foll:

14 • NEXT ROW (DEC; RS): Patt to last 2 (2, 3, 3, 4, 4, 5) sts, turn. Rem sts unworked. [67 (75, 78, 82, 85, 91, 94) sts]

Note: To ensure an even raglan edge that will be easy to seam, work 1 sc in third and third-to-last st of all dec rows. On RS rows worked even, work 1 sc in each of first 3 and last 3 sts in row.

15 • NEXT ROW (DEC): Ch 1, sc2tog, patt as established to last 4 (4, 5, 5, 6, 6, 7) sts, sc2tog, turn. Rem sts unworked. [63 (71, 73, 77, 79, 85, 87) sts]

16 • NEXT ROW (DEC): Ch 1, sc2tog, sc in next st, patt as established to last 3 sts, sc in next st, sc2tog, turn. [61 (69, 71, 75, 77, 83, 85) sts]

17 • Rep step 16 (last row) 0 (2, 2, 2, 0, 2, 0) more times. [61 (65, 67, 71, 77, 79, 85) sts]

18 • NEXT ROW: Ch 1, sc in each of first 2 sts, patt as established to last 2 sts, sc in each of last 2 sts, turn.

NEXT ROW (DEC): Ch 1, sc2tog, sc in next st, patt as established to last 3 sts, sc in next st, sc2tog, turn. [59 (63, 65, 69, 75, 77, 83) sts]

19 • Rep step 18 (last 2 rows) 1 (0, 0, 0, 1, 0, 1) more time. [57 (63, 65, 69, 73, 77, 81) sts]

20 • With A and working all rows in sc sts, rep step 18 once more. [55 (61, 63, 67, 71, 75, 79) sts]

TWIN POSTS YOKE

21 • NEXT ROW (WS): Ch 1, sc in each of first 5 (5, 3, 5, 4, 3, 8) sts, pm, sc in each st to last 5 (5, 3, 5, 4, 3, 8) sts, pm, sc in each st to end, turn.

22 • NEXT ROW (DEC): Ch 1, sc2tog, sc in each st to marker, sc in each of next 3 sts, *FPDC around next sc in row below, sc in next st, FPDC around next sc in row below, sc in each of next 3 sts*, rep from * to * to next marker, sc in each st to last 2 sts, sc2tog, turn. [53 (59, 61, 65, 69, 73, 77) sts]

23 • NEXT ROW: Ch 1, sc in first and each st to end, turn.

NEXT ROW (DEC): Ch 1, sc2tog, sc in each st to marker, sc in each of first 3 sts, *FPDC around next FPDC in row below, sc in next st, FPDC around next FPDC in row below, sc in each of next 3 sts*, rep from * to * to marker, sc in each st to last 2 sts, sc2tog, turn. [51 (57, 59, 63, 67, 71, 75) sts]

24 • Rep step 23 (last 2 rows) 13 (15, 16, 17, 18, 19, 20) more times. Fasten off. [25 (27, 27, 29, 31, 33, 35) sts]

Front

1 • Work as for back to step 24. [51 (57, 59, 63, 67, 71, 75) sts]

2 • Rep back, step 23, for 6 (8, 8, 9, 10, 10, 11) more times. [39 (41, 43, 45, 47, 51, 53) sts]

RIGHT SHOULDER SHAPING

3 • NEXT ROW (DEC; WS): Ch 1, sc in each of first 2 sts, patt as established across next 11 (11, 13, 13, 15, 15) sts, sc2tog, turn. Rem sts unworked. [14 (14, 16, 16, 16, 18, 18) sts]

4 • NEXT ROW (DEC): Ch 1, sc2tog, sc in next st, patt as established to last 3 sts, sc in next st, sc2tog, turn. [12 (12, 14, 14, 14, 16, 16) sts]

NEXT ROW: Ch 1, sc in each of first 2 sts, patt as established to last 2 sts, sc in each of last 2 sts, turn.

5 • Rep step 4 (last 2 rows) 4 (4, 5, 5, 5, 6, 6) more times. [4 sts]

6 • NEXT ROW (DEC): Ch 1, sc2tog twice, turn. [2 sts]

7 • NEXT ROW: Ch 1, sc in each st, turn.

8 • NEXT ROW (DEC): Ch 1, sc2tog. Fasten off.

LEFT SHOULDER SHAPING

9 • With WS facing, working into last full-width row and starting at inner right front shoulder shaping, sk next 9 (11, 9, 11, 13, 13, 15) sts. Join yarn with sc2tog (count as st) and working in st patt as established on last full-width row, cont as follows:

NEXT ROW (WS): Patt as established to last 2 sts, sc in each of last 2 sts, turn. [14 (14, 16, 16, 16, 18, 18) sts]

10 • NEXT ROW (DEC): Ch 1, sc2tog, sc in next st, patt as established to last 3 sc, sc in next st, sc2tog, turn. [12 (12, 14, 14, 14, 16, 16) sts]

NEXT ROW: Ch 1, sc in each of first 2 sts, patt as established to last 2 sts, sc in each of last 2 sts, turn.

11 • Rep step 10 (last 2 rows) 4 (4, 5, 5, 5, 6, 6) more times. [4 sts]

12 • NEXT ROW (DEC): Ch 1, sc2tog twice, turn. [2 sts]

13 • NEXT ROW: Ch 1, sc in each st, turn.

14 • NEXT ROW (DEC): Ch 1, sc2tog. Fasten off.

Sleeve (Make 2)

1 • Ch 26 (28, 30, 30, 32, 34, 36).

FOUNDATION ROW (WS): Sc in 2nd ch from hk (count as st) and in each ch to end. [25 (27, 29, 29, 31, 33, 35) sts]

2 • ROWS 2 AND 3: Ch 1, sc in first and each st to end, turn.

3 • ROW 4: Ch 1, sc in first 2 (0, 1, 1, 2, 0, 1) sts, pm, sc in each of next 3 sts, *FPDC around next sc in row below, sc in next st, FPDC around next sc in row below, sc in each of next 3 sts*, rep from * to * to last 2 (0, 1, 1, 2, 0, 1) sts, pm, sc in each st to end, turn.

4 • ROW 5: Ch 1, sc in first and each st to end, turn.

5 • ROW 6 (INC): Ch 1, 2 sc in first st, sc in each st to marker, *sc in each of next 3 sts, *FPDC around next FPDC in row below, sc in next st, FPDC around next FPDC in row below, sc in each of next 3 sts*, rep from * to * to marker, sc in each st to last st, 2 sc in last st, turn. [27 (29, 31, 31, 33, 35, 37) sts]

6 • ROWS 7 AND 9: Ch 1, sc in first and each st to end, turn.

ROW 8: Ch 1, sc in first and each st to marker, sc in each of next 3 sts, *FPDC around next FPDC in row below, sc in next st, FPDC around next FPDC in row below, sc in each of next 3 sts*, rep from * to * to marker, sc in each st to end, turn.

ROW 10 (INC): As step 5. [29 (31, 33, 33, 35, 37, 39) sts]

7 • Rep step 6 (last 4 rows) 10 (12, 13, 14, 14, 15, 15) more times. [49 (55, 59, 61, 63, 67, 69) sts]

8 • Work even in st patt as established until 14 (14½, 15, 15, 15½, 16, 16½)" from beg, ending with RS row complete. Remove markers.

COLORED PEBBLES BAND

9 • Work as for back Colored Pebbles band steps 5–13. (See page 61.)

RAGLAN SHAPING

10 • Rep Colored Pebbles band, steps 6–12, and AT THE SAME TIME shape work as for back raglan shaping, steps 14–17. [41 (43, 45, 47, 51, 51, 55) sts]

11 • Cont in Colored Pebbles band to end of step 12, then working rows of sc, shape work as foll:

NEXT ROW (WS): Ch 1, sc in each of first 2 sts, patt as established to last 2 sts, sc in each of last 2 sts, turn.

NEXT ROW (DEC): Ch 1, sc2tog, sc in next st, patt as established to last 3 sts, sc in next st, sc2tog, turn. [39 (41, 43, 45, 49, 49, 53) sts]

12 • Rep step 11 (last 2 rows) 1 (0, 0, 0, 1, 0, 1) more time. [37 (41, 43, 45, 47, 49, 51) sts]

13 • With A, rep step 11 once more. [35 (39, 41, 43, 45, 47, 49) sts]

TWIN POSTS UPPER SLEEVE

14 • NEXT ROW (WS): Ch 1, sc in each of first 7 (6, 7, 8, 3, 7, 8) sts, pm, sc in each st to last 7 (6, 7, 8, 3, 7, 8) sts, pm, sc in each st to end, turn.

15 • NEXT ROW (DEC): Ch 1, sc2tog, sc in each st to marker, sc in each of first 3 sts, *FPDC around next sc in row below, sc in next st, FPDC around next sc in row below, sc in each of next 3 sts*, rep from * to * to next marker, sc in each st to last 2 sts, sc2tog, turn. [33 (37, 39, 41, 43, 45, 47) sts]

Starting with row 5, work Twin Posts st patt as foll:

16 • NEXT ROW: Ch 1, sc in first and each st to first marker, patt as established to next marker, sc in each st to end, turn.

NEXT ROW (DEC): Ch 1, sc2tog, sc in each st to marker, patt as established to next marker, sc in each st to last 2 sts, sc2tog, turn. [31 (35, 37, 39, 41, 43, 45) sts]

17 • Rep step 16 (last 2 rows) 13 (15, 16, 17, 18, 19, 20) more times. Fasten off. [5 sts]

Finishing

1 • Place 1 sleeve's diagonal raglan edge along corresponding edge of front. With WS tog at beg at neck, sew edges with rows matching. Continue seam by sewing rem portion of body's raglan edge to short, horizontal row at beg of sleeve shaping.

2 • Sew rem raglan sleeve edge to back in same manner. Sew rem sleeve to body in same manner.

3 • Sew back to front at sides and underarms.

Neckband

1 • With A and RS facing, beg at top of left front neck, join with sc (count as st), and work evenly spaced sts as foll:

ROW 1 (RS): LEFT FRONT SLOPE: 11 (11, 13, 13, 13, 15, 15) sc;
FRONT NECK BASE: 9 (11, 9, 11, 13, 13, 15) sc;
RIGHT FRONT SLOPE: 12 (12, 14, 14, 14, 16, 16) sc;
RIGHT SLEEVE TOP: 3 sc;
BACK NECK: 20 (22, 22, 24, 24, 26, 28) sc;
LEFT SLEEVE TOP: 3 sc. [59 (63, 65, 69, 71, 77, 81) sts]
Fasten off. Do not turn.

2 • Row 2 (RS): With RS facing and B, join yarn with sc (count as st) in first sc of row 1 (at top of left front neck), sc in each st to end, turn.

3 • Row 3: With D, ch 1, sc in first st, *hdc in next st, sl st in next st, rep from * to * to last 2 sts, hdc in next st, sc in last st, turn.

4 • Row 4: With B, ch 1, sc in first st and each st to end. Fasten off. Do not turn.

5 • Row 5: With RS facing and A, join yarn with sc (count as st) in first sc of row 4 (at top of left front neck), sc in each st to end. Fasten off.

6 • With RS tog, sew collar at left shoulder.

Clover Panel

S-Cable Panel

Celtic Garden

Lush with pattern and texture, this cardigan cultivates a beautiful array of stitches. Bobbles, cables, and posts merge, shift, and punctuate the surface with controlled abandon. While there are only two stitch patterns, the clover and the S-cable, the pattern is meant to challenge. More than one stitch pattern is worked across every row and there are many different stitches in the same row. To balance this hard work, the garment shapes are simple.

YARN

Classic Wool Merino from Patons, color #77023 Camel

Extra Small	•	9 balls
Small	•	9 balls
Medium	•	9 balls
Large	•	9 balls
Extra Large	•	10 balls

SUPPLIES

7 (4.5 mm) crochet hook
H/8 (5 mm) crochet hook
6 stitch markers

GAUGE

7 sts and 8 rows to 2" in Clover panel with H/8 (5 mm) hook

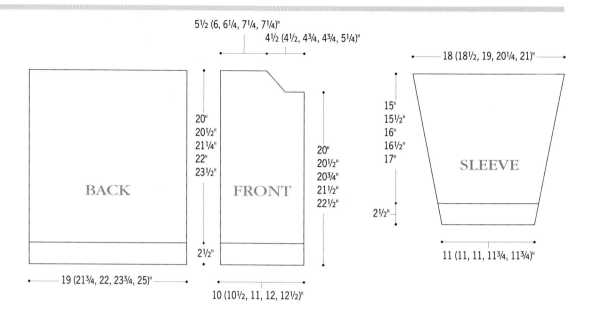

SIZING	Extra Small	Small	Medium	Large	Extra Large
To fit bust	31½"	34¼"	37¼"	41"	43¼"
*Finished bust**	40½"	44¼"	45½"	49¼"	51½"
Shoulder width	5½"	6"	6¼"	7¼"	7¼"
Sleeve length	17½"	18"	18½"	19"	19½"
Center back length	22½"	23"	23¾"	24½"	26"

*Measurement of buttoned garment.

S-CABLE PANEL

Worked over 6 sts (also add 1 ch for base ch)

FOUNDATION ROW (RS): Sc in 2nd ch from hk (count as st) and in each ch to end, turn.

ROW 2: Ch 1, sc in first and each st to end, turn.

ROW 3: Ch 1, sc in first st, FPDC around each of next 4 sc in row below (second, third, fourth, and fifth sts from edge or st marker), sc in last st, turn.

ROW 4 AND ALL WS ROWS: Ch 1, sc in first st and each st to end, turn.

ROW 5: Ch 1, sc in first st, cb4, sc in last st, turn.

ROW 7: Ch 1, sc in first st, FPDC around each of next 4 FPTR, sc in last st, turn.

ROW 9: Ch 1, sc in first st, cb4R, sc in last st, turn.

ROW 11: Ch 1, sc in first st, FPDC around each of next 4 FPTR, sc in last st, turn.

Rows 4–11 form S-Cable panel.

CLOVER PANEL

Worked over 7 sts (also add 1 ch for base ch)

FOUNDATION ROW (RS): Sc in 2nd ch from hk (count as st) and in each ch to end, turn.

ROWS 2 AND 3: Ch 1, sc in first and each st to end, turn.

ROW 4: Ch 1, sc in each of first 3 sts, bobble in next st, sc in each of last 3 sts, turn.

ROW 5: Ch 1, sc in each st to end, turn.

ROW 6: Ch 1, sc in first st, bobble in next st, sc in each of next 3 sts, bobble in next st, sc in last st, turn.

ROW 7: Ch 1, sc in first and each st to end, turn.

ROW 8: Ch 1, sc in each of first 3 sts, bobble in next st, sc in each of last 3 sts, turn.

ROW 9: Ch 1, sc in first and each st to end, turn.

Rows 2–9 form Clover panel.

Back

1 • With smaller hk, ch 68 (74, 78, 84, 88).

FOUNDATION ROW (RS): Sc in 2nd ch from hk (count as st) and in each ch to end, turn. [67 (73, 77, 83, 87) sc]

MOCK POST RIBBING

2 • Row 2 (WS): Ch 1, sc in first and each st to end, turn.

3 • Row 3: Ch 1, sc in first st, FPDC around next sc in row below, *sc in next st, FPDC around sc in row below*, rep from * to * to last st, sc in last st, turn.

4 • Row 4: Ch 1, sc in first and each st to end, turn.

Row 5: Ch 1, sc in first st, FPDC around next FPDC, *sc in next st, FPDC around next FPDC*, rep from * to * to last st, sc in last st, turn.

5 • Rep step 4 (last 2 rows) until 2½" from beg, ending with WS row complete.

BODY

6 • Change to larger hk.

Next Row (RS): Ch 1, sc in first and each st to end, turn.

7 • Next Row: Ch 1, sc in each of first 0 (3, 5, 8, 10) sts, *pm, sc in next 15 sts*, rep from * to * 3 more times, pm, sc in next 7 sts, pm, sc in each st to end.

Note: In foll steps, Extra Small sk left and right borders.

8 • Next Row: Right Border: Ch 1, sc in first and each st to marker;

Clover Panel: Sc in each of next 7 sts;

Post Stitch: *FPDC around next sc in row below;

S-Cable Panel: Sc in next st, FPDC around each of next 4 sc in row below, sc in next st;

Post Stitch: FPDC around next sc in row below;

Clover Panel: Sc in each of next 7 sts*;

Continue Panels: Rep from * to * 3 more times;

Left Border: Sc in each st to end, turn.

9 • Next Row: Border: Ch 1, sc in first and each st to marker;

Clover: *Sc in each of next 3 sts, bobble in next st, sc in each of next 3 sts;

Post: Sc in next st;

S-Cable: Sc in each of next 6 sts;

Post: Sc in next st*;

Continue Panels: Rep from * to * 3 more times;

Clover: Sc in each of next 3 sts, bobble in next st, sc in each of next 3 sts;

Border: Sc in each st to end, turn.

10 • Starting with row 5 of Clover panel (see previous page) and row 5 of S-Cable panel (see previous page), cont in panels and borders as established until 22½ (23, 23¾, 24½, 26)" from beg. Fasten off.

Left Front

1 • With smaller hk, ch 36 (38, 40, 43, 45).

Foundation Row (WS): Sc in 2nd ch from hk (count as st) and in each ch to end, turn. [35 (37, 39, 42, 44) sc]

2 • Work as for back Mock Post Ribbing, steps 2–5.

BODY

3 • Change to larger hk.

Next Row (RS): Ch 1, sc in first and each st to end, turn.

4 • NEXT ROW: Ch 1, sc in first 3 sts, *pm, sc in next 15 sts*, rep from * to * once more, pm, sc in each st to end, turn.

5 • NEXT ROW: SIDE BORDER: Ch 1, sc in first and each st to marker;

POST: *FPDC around next sc in row below;

CLOVER: Sc in each of next 7 sts;

POST: FPDC around next sc in row below;

S-CABLE: Sc in next st, FPDC around each of next 4 sc in row below, sc in next st*;

CONTINUE PANELS: Rep from * to * once more;

POST: FPDC around next st in row below;

FRONT BORDER: Sc in each of last 2 sts, turn.

6 • NEXT ROW: FRONT BORDER: Ch 1, sc in each of first 2 sts;

POST: Sc in next st;

S-CABLE: *Sc in each of next 6 sts;

POST: Sc in next st;

CLOVER: Sc in each of next 3 sts, bobble in next st, sc in each of next 3 sts;

POST: Sc in next st*;

CONTINUE PANELS: Rep from * to * once more;

SIDE BORDER: Sc in each st to end, turn.

7 • Starting with row 5 of Clover panel and row 5 of S-Cable panel, cont in borders and panels as established until 20 (20½, 20¾, 21½, 22½)" from beg, ending with WS row complete.

LEFT NECK SHAPING

8 • NEXT ROW (DEC; RS): Patt as established across first 25 (27, 28, 31, 31) sts, sc in next st, sc2tog, turn. Rem sts unworked. [27 (29, 30, 33, 33) sts]

9 • NEXT ROW (DEC): Ch 1, sc2tog, sc in next st, patt as established to end, turn. [26 (28, 29, 32, 32) sts]

NEXT ROW: Patt as established to last 3 sts, sc in next st, sc2tog, turn. [25 (27, 28, 31, 31) sts]

10 • Rep step 9 (last 2 rows) 3 more times. [19 (21, 22, 25, 25) sts]

11 • Work even in border and panels as established until 22½ (23, 23¾, 24½, 26)" from beg of ribbing. Remove markers. Fasten off.

Right Front

1 • With smaller hk, ch 36 (38, 40, 43, 45).

FOUNDATION ROW (WS): Sc in 2nd ch from hk (count as st) and in each ch to end, turn. [35 (37, 39, 42, 44) sc]

2 • Work as for back Mock Post Ribbing, steps 2–5.

BODY

3 • Change to larger hk.

NEXT ROW (RS): Ch 1, sc in first and each st to end, turn.

4 • NEXT ROW: Ch 1, sc in first 2 (4, 6, 9, 11) sts, pm, *sc in next 15 sts, pm*, rep from * to * once more, sc in each st to end, turn.

5 • NEXT ROW: FRONT BORDER: Ch 1, sc in each of first 2 sts;

POST STITCH: FPDC around next sc in row below;

S-CABLE PANEL: *Sc in next st, FPDC around each of next 4 sc in row below, sc in next st;

POST STITCH: FPDC around next sc in row below;

CLOVER PANEL: Sc in each of next 7 sts;

POST STITCH: FPDC around next st in row below*, rep from * to * once more;

SIDE BORDER: Sc in each st to end, turn.

6 • NEXT ROW: BORDER: Ch 1, sc in first and each st to marker;

POST: *Sc in next st;

CLOVER: Sc in each of next 3 sts, bobble in next st, sc in each of next 3 sts;

POST: Sc in next st;

S-CABLE: Sc in each of next 6 sts*, rep from * to * once more;

POST: Sc in next st;

BORDER: Sc in each of last 2 sts, turn.

7 • Starting with row 5 of Clover panel and row 5 of S-Cable panel, cont in borders and panels as established until 20 (20½, 20¾, 21½, 22½)" from beg, ending with RS row complete.

RIGHT NECK SHAPING

8 • NEXT ROW (DEC; WS): Patt as established across first 25 (27, 28, 31, 31) sts, sc in next st, sc2tog, turn. Rem sts unworked. [27 (29, 30, 33, 33) sts]

9 • Work as for Left Neck Shaping, steps 9–11.

Sleeve (Make 2)

1 • With smaller hk, ch 36.

FOUNDATION ROW (WS): Sc in 2nd ch from hk (count as st) and in each ch to end. [35 sts]

RIBBING

2 • Work as for back Mock Post Ribbing, steps 2–5.

BODY

3 • Change to larger hk.

NEXT ROW (RS): Ch 1, sc in each of first 3 (3, 3, 2, 2) sts, *2 sc in next st, sc in each of next 8 (8, 8, 5, 5) sts*, rep from * to * 2 (2, 2, 4, 4) more times, 2 sc in next st, sc in each of last 4 (4, 4, 2, 2) sts, turn. [39 (39, 39, 41, 41) sts]

4 • **NEXT ROW:** Ch 1, sc in first 1 (1, 1, 2, 2) st, pm, *sc in each of next 15 sts, pm,* rep from * to * once more, sc in each of next 7 sts, pm, sc in each st to end, turn.

5 • **NEXT ROW: BORDER:** Ch 1, sc in first and each st to marker;

CLOVER: Sc in each of next 7 sts;

POST: *FPDC around next sc in row below;

S-CABLE: Sc in next st, FPDC around each of next 4 sc in row below, sc in next st;

POST: FPDC around next sc in row below;

CLOVER: Sc in each of next 7 sts*;

CONTINUE PANELS: Rep from * to * once more;

BORDER: Sc in each st to end, turn.

6 • **NEXT ROW (INC): BORDER:** 2 sc in first st, sc in each st to marker;

CLOVER: *Sc in each of first 3 sts, bobble in next st, sc in each of next 3 sts;

POST: Sc in next st;

S-CABLE: Sc in each of next 6 sts;

POST: Sc in next st*;

CONTINUE PANELS: Rep from * to * once more;

CLOVER: Sc in each of first 3 sts, bobble in next st, sc in each of next 3 sts;

BORDER: Sc in each st to last st, 2 sc in last st, turn. [41 (41, 41, 43, 43) sts]

Starting with row 5 of Clover panel and row 5 of S-Cable panel and maintaining sc borders, cont as foll:

7 • Work 3 rows even in st patts as established.

NEXT ROW (INC): Ch 1, 2 sc in first st, patt as established to last st, 2 sc in last st, turn. [43 (43, 43, 45, 45) sts]

8 • Rep step 7 (last 4 rows) 10 (11, 12, 13, 14) more times. [63 (65, 67, 71, 73) sts]

9 • Work even in borders and panels as established until 17½ (18, 18½, 19, 19½)" from beg. Remove markers. Fasten off.

Neckband

1 • Sew back to front at both shoulders.

2 • With smaller hk, join yarn at center front of right neck edge with sc (count as st), and work evenly spaced sts as foll:

ROW 1 (RS): RIGHT FRONT: 16 (16, 18, 18, 20) sc;

BACK NECK: 25 (25, 27, 27, 29) sc;

LEFT FRONT: 16 (16, 18, 18, 20) sc. [57 (57, 63, 63, 69) sts]

3 • Work as for back Mock Post Ribbing, steps 2–5, until 1½" from beg of neckband. Fasten off.

Button Band

1 • With smaller hk, join yarn with sc (count as st) at top corner of left front neck and work evenly spaced sts as foll:

ROW 1 (RS): 71 (73, 73, 77, 77) sc down left front cardigan edge to bottom edge.

2 • Work as for back Mock Post Ribbing, steps 2–5, until 1½" from beg. Fasten off.

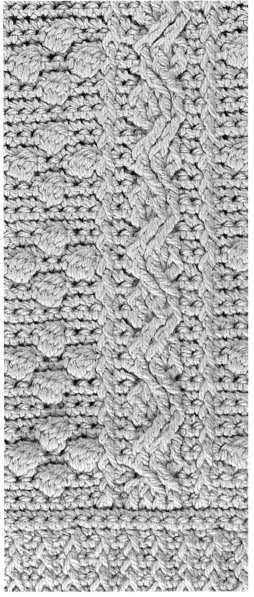

Celtic Garden

Buttonhole Band

1 • With smaller hk, join yarn with sc (count as st) at bottom corner of right front and work evenly spaced sts as foll:

Row 1 (RS) : 71 (73, 73, 77, 77) sc up right front edge to neck.

2 • Work as for back Mock Post Ribbing, steps 2 and 3.

3 • **Row 4:** Ch 1, sc in each of first 2 (3, 3, 2, 2) sts, *ch 3, sk next 2 sts, sc in each of next 11 (11, 11, 12, 12) sts*, rep from * to * 4 more times, ch 3, sk next 2 sts, sc in each of last 2 (3, 3, 3, 3) sts, turn.

4 • **Row 5:** Work Mock Post Ribbing st patt as established, working 2 sc into each ch-3 lp.

5 • **Row 6:** Sc in first and each st to end.

6 • **Row 7:** Cont Mock Post Ribbing st patt as established, working FPDC around sc in row below at buttonhole.

7 • Cont in Mock Post Ribbing until 1½" from beg.

Finishing

1 • Sew buttons on left front to correspond with right front buttonholes.

2 • On front and back, place markers at each side (vertical edge) 9 (9¼, 9½, 10, 10½)" below shoulder seam. Sew sleeves into body between markers. (See "Inserting Sleeves" on page 93.)

3 • Sew back to front at sides and underarms.

Alpine Meadow

A cozy hood and a zippered front are sure to keep the cold at bay when you explore the outdoors. Sporty stripes, worked with only one color in each row, are made with a simple 4-row repeat that's a walk in the park. Likewise, the braided posts on the lower body and sleeves have only one post cross in each row. The jaunty border is stitched at the beginning of each garment piece and the hood is stitched onto the neck after the shoulders are seamed.

YARN

Wool-Ease Worsted Weight from Lion Brand

Color A: #115 Blue Mist

Extra Small	•	9 balls
Small	•	10 balls
Medium	•	10 balls
Large	•	11 balls
Extra Large	•	12 balls

Color B: #130 Green Heather

All Sizes • 2 balls

Color C: #139 Dark Rose Heather

All Sizes • 2 balls

Color D: #151 Grey Heather

All Sizes • 2 balls

Supplies and gauge on the next page.

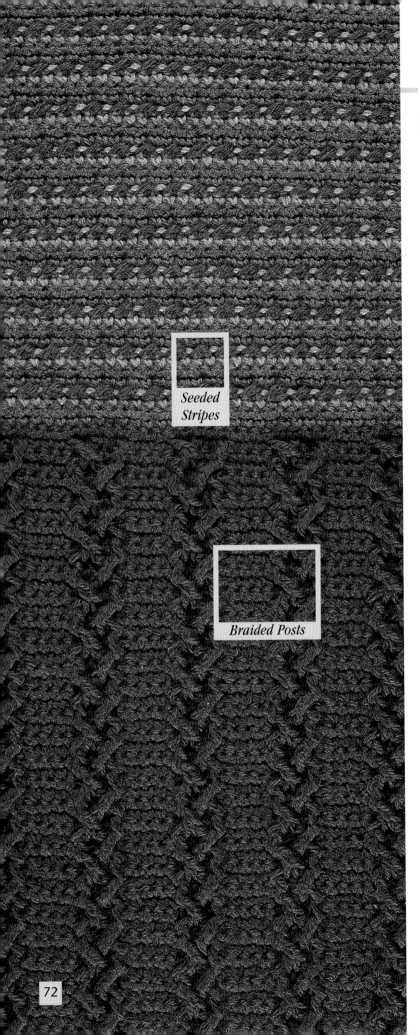

Seeded Stripes

Braided Posts

SUPPLIES

- H/8 (5 mm) crochet hook
- 4 stitch markers
- 22 (22, 22, 24, 24)" separating zipper*
- All-purpose sewing thread in color matched to color A yarn
- Hand-sewing needle
- Quilter's straight pins (1¼" long, with large head)

Buy the zipper after assembling the garment pieces so that you'll know the exact length required.

GAUGE

16 sts and 17 rows to 4" in Braided Posts st patt

16 sts and 19 rows to 4" in Seeded Stripes st patt

BRAIDED POSTS STITCH PATTERN

Multiple of 8 sts + 3 sts (also add 1 ch for base ch)

FOUNDATION ROW (RS): Sc in 2nd ch from hk (count as st) and in each ch to end, turn.

ROW 2: Ch 1, sc in first and each st to end, turn.

ROW 3: Ch 1, sc first 3 sts, *FPDC around next sc in row below (fourth st from edge or last FPDC), sc in next st, FPDC around next sc in row below (second st from last FPDC), sc in next st, FPDC around next sc in row below (second st from last FPDC), sc in each of next 3 sts*, rep from * to * to end, turn.

ROW 4: Ch 1, sc in first and each st to end, turn.

ROW 5: Ch 1, sc first 3 sts, *FPDC around next post st in row below, sc in next st, cr3, sc in each of next 3 sts*, rep from * to * to end, turn.

ROW 6: Ch 1, sc in first and each st to end, turn.

ROW 7: Ch 1, sc in first 3 sts, *cr3R, sc in next st, FPDC around next post st in row below, sc in each of next 3 sts*, rep from * to * to end, turn.

Rows 4–7 form Braided Posts st patt rep.

SEEDED STRIPES STITCH PATTERN

Multiple of 2 sts + 1 st (also add 1 ch for base ch)

FOUNDATION ROW (RS): With A, sc in 2nd ch from hk (count as st) and in each ch to end, turn.

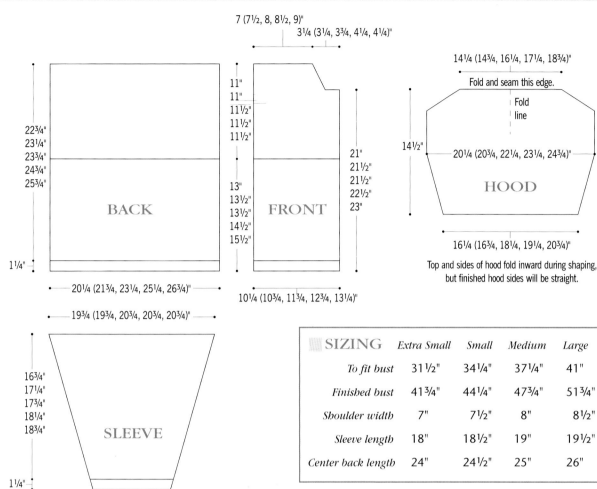

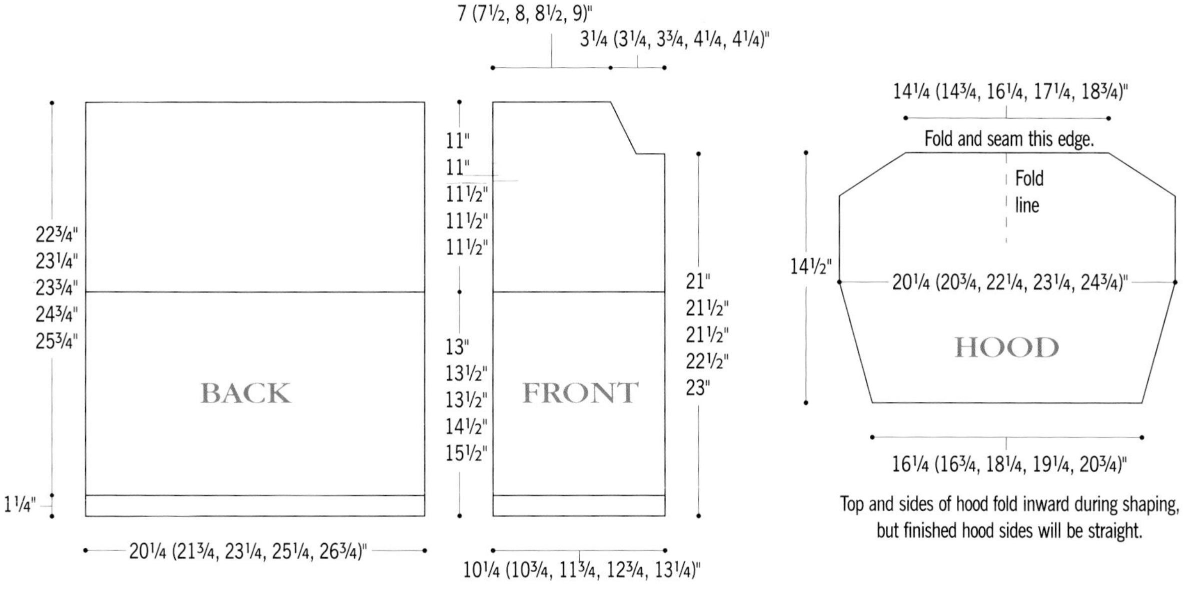
7 (7 1/2, 8, 8 1/2, 9)"
3 1/4 (3 1/4, 3 3/4, 4 1/4, 4 1/4)"
BACK
22 3/4" 23 1/4" 23 3/4" 24 3/4" 25 3/4"
1 1/4"
20 1/4 (21 3/4, 23 1/4, 25 1/4, 26 3/4)"
FRONT
11" 11" 11 1/2" 11 1/2" 11 1/2"
13" 13 1/2" 13 1/2" 14 1/2" 15 1/2"
21" 21 1/2" 21 1/2" 22 1/2" 23"
10 1/4 (10 3/4, 11 3/4, 12 3/4, 13 1/4)"
14 1/4 (14 3/4, 16 1/4, 17 1/4, 18 3/4)"
Fold and seam this edge.
Fold line
14 1/2"
20 1/4 (20 3/4, 22 1/4, 23 1/4, 24 3/4)"
HOOD
16 1/4 (16 3/4, 18 1/4, 19 1/4, 20 3/4)"
Top and sides of hood fold inward during shaping, but finished hood sides will be straight.

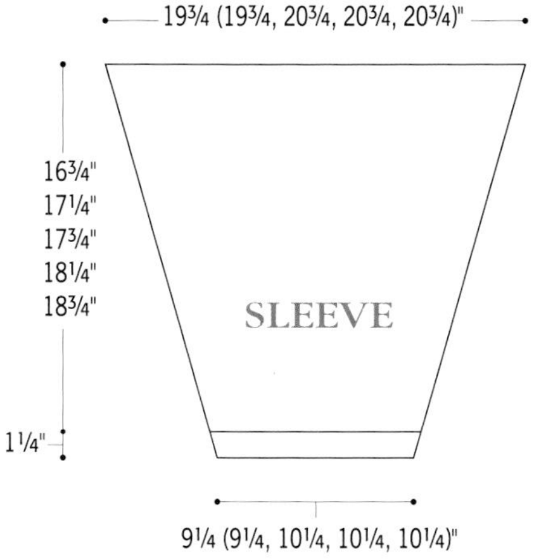
19 3/4 (19 3/4, 20 3/4, 20 3/4, 20 3/4)"
16 3/4" 17 1/4" 17 3/4" 18 1/4" 18 3/4"
SLEEVE
1 1/4"
9 1/4 (9 1/4, 10 1/4, 10 1/4, 10 1/4)"

SIZING	Extra Small	Small	Medium	Large	Extra Large
To fit bust	31 1/2"	34 1/4"	37 1/4"	41"	43 1/4"
Finished bust	41 3/4"	44 1/4"	47 3/4"	51 3/4"	54 1/4"
Shoulder width	7"	7 1/2"	8"	8 1/2"	9"
Sleeve length	18"	18 1/2"	19"	19 1/2"	20"
Center back length	24"	24 1/2"	25"	26"	27"

Row 2: With A, ch 1, sc in first st, *hdc in next st, sl st loosely in next st*, rep from * to * to last 2 sts, hdc in next st, sc in last st, turn.

Row 3: With B, ch 1, sc in first and each st to end, turn.

Row 4: With C, ch 1, sc in first and each st to end, turn.

Row 5: With D, ch 1, sc in first and each st to end, turn.

Rows 2–5 form Seeded Stripes st patt rep.

Back

1 • With A, ch 82 (88, 94, 102, 108).

Foundation Row (WS): Sc in 2nd ch from hk (count as st) and in each ch to end, turn. [81 (87, 93, 101, 107) sc]

MULTICOLORED BORDER

2 • **Row 2 (RS):** With B, ch 1, sc in each st to end, turn.

3 • Rep last step (row 2) 3 more times, changing color for each row and working in foll color sequence: C, D, A.

BODY

With A only, cont as foll:

4 • **Row 6 (RS):** Ch 1, sc in each st to end, turn.

5 • **Row 7:** Ch 1, sc first 3 (2, 1, 1, 0) sts, pm, sc in each st to last 3 (2, 1, 1, 0) sts, pm, sc in each st to end, turn.

6 • **Row 8:** Ch 1, sc in first and each st to marker, sc in each of next 3 sts, *FPDC around next sc in row below, sc in next st, FPDC around next sc in row below, sc in next st, FPDC around next sc in row below, sc in each of next 3 sts*, rep from * to * to marker, sc in each st to end, turn.

7 • Starting with row 4 of Braided Posts st patt (see page 72), work even until 13 (13½, 13½, 14½, 15½)" from beg, ending with RS row complete. Remove markers.

SEEDED STRIPES YOKE

8 • NEXT ROW (WS): Ch 1, sc in first and each st to end, turn.

9 • With B and starting with row 3 of Seeded Stripes st patt (see page 73), work even until 24 (24½, 25, 26, 27)" from beg. Fasten off.

Left Front

1 • With A, ch 42 (44, 48, 52, 54).

FOUNDATION ROW (WS): Sc in 2nd ch from hk (count as st) and in each ch to end, turn. [41 (43, 47, 51, 53) sc]

2 • Work as for back Multicolored border, steps 2 and 3.

BODY

With A only, cont as foll:

3 • ROW 6 (RS): Ch 1, sc in first and each st to end, turn.

4 • ROW 7: Ch 1, sc in first and each st to last 6 (0, 4, 0, 2) sts, pm, sc in each st to end, turn.

Note: Beg of row 7 is center front. Single crochet border established on 6 (0, 4, 0, 2) sts, between marker and side edge.

5 • ROW 8: Ch 1, sc in first and each st to marker, sc in each of next 3 sts, *FPDC around next sc in row below, sc in next st, FPDC around next sc in row below, sc in next st, FPDC around next sc in row below, sc in each of next 3 sts*, rep from * to * end, turn.

6 • Starting with row 4 of Braided Posts st patt (see page 72), cont in st patt as established between center front and marker and working sc between marker and side edge, work even until 13 (13½, 13½, 14½, 15½)" from beg, ending RS row complete. Remove marker.

SEEDED STRIPES YOKE

7 • NEXT ROW (WS): Ch 1, sc in first and each st to end, turn.

8 • Starting with B and row 3 of Seeded Stripes st patt, work even until 21 (21½, 21½, 22½, 23)" from beg, ending with WS row complete.

LEFT NECK SHAPING

9 • NEXT ROW (DEC; RS): Patt as established to last 8 sts, sc2tog, turn. Rem sts unworked. [34 (36, 40, 44, 46) sts]

10 • NEXT ROW (DEC): Ch 1, sc2tog, patt as established to end, turn. [33 (35, 39, 43, 45) sts]

NEXT ROW (DEC): Patt as established to last 2 sts, sc2tog, turn. [32 (34, 38, 42, 44) sts]

11 • Rep step 10 (last 2 rows) 2 (2, 3, 4, 4) more times. [28 (30, 32, 34, 36) sts]

12 • Work even in st patt as established until 24 (24½, 25, 26, 27)" from beg. Fasten off.

Right Front

1 • Work as for left front, steps 1–3.

2 • ROW 7 (WS): Ch 1, sc first 6 (0, 4, 0, 2) sts, pm, sc in each st to end, turn.

Note: End of row 7 is center front. Single crochet border established on 6 (0, 4, 0, 2) sts, between marker and side edge.

3 • ROW 8: Ch 1, sc in first 3 sts, *FPDC around next sc in row below, sc in next st, FPDC around next sc in row below, sc in next st, FPDC around next sc in row below, sc in each of next 3 sts*, rep from * to * to marker, sc in each st to end, turn. [41 (43, 47, 51, 53) sts]

4 • Cont in Braided Posts st patt as established (starting with row 4) working sc between side edge and marker, then stitch patt to marker between center front edge, work even until 13 (13½, 13½, 14½, 15½)" from beg, ending with RS row complete. Remove marker.

SEEDED STRIPES YOKE

5 • NEXT ROW (WS): Ch 1, sc in first and each st to end, turn.

6 • Starting with B and row 3 of Seeded Stripes st patt work even until 21 (21½, 21½, 22½, 23)" from beg, ending with WS row complete.

RIGHT NECK SHAPING

7 • NEXT ROW (DEC; RS): Ch 1, sl st in each of first 6 sts, pm, sc2tog, patt as previously established to end. [34 (36, 40, 44, 46) sts]

8 • NEXT ROW (DEC): Patt as established to last 2 sts (before marker, first time worked), sc2tog, turn. [33 (35, 39, 43, 45) sts]

NEXT ROW (DEC): Ch 1, sc2tog, patt as established to end, turn. [32 (34, 38, 42, 44) sts]

9 • Remove marker. Rep step 8 (last 2 rows) 2 (2, 3, 4, 4) more times. [28 (30, 32, 34, 36) sts]

10 • Work even in st patt as established until 24 (24½, 25, 26, 27)" from beg. Fasten off.

Sleeve (Make 2)

1 • With A, ch 38 (38, 42, 42, 42).

FOUNDATION ROW (WS): Sc in 2nd ch from hk (count as st) and in each ch to end, turn. [37 (37, 41, 41, 41) sts]

BORDER

2 • Work as for back Multicolored border, steps 2 and 3.

BODY

With A only, cont as foll:

3 • ROW 6 (INC; RS): Ch 1, 2 sc in first st, sc in each st to last st, 2 sc in last st, turn. [39 (39, 43, 43, 43) sts]

4 • ROW 7: Ch 1, sc first 2 (2, 0, 0, 0) sts, pm, sc in each st to last 2 (2, 0, 0, 0) sts, pm, sc in each st to end, turn.

5 • ROW 8 (INC): Ch 1, 2 sc in first st, sc in each st to marker, sc in each of next 3 sts, *FPDC around next sc in row below, sc in next st, FPDC around next sc in row below, sc in next st, FPDC around next sc in row below, sc in each of next 3 sts*, rep from * to * to marker, sc in each st to last st, 2 sc in last st, turn. [41 (41, 45, 45, 45) sts]

Starting with row 4, cont in Braided Posts st patt as established between markers and inc as foll:

6 • NEXT ROW: Ch 1, sc in first and each st to marker, patt as established to next marker, sc in each st to end, turn.

NEXT ROW (INC): Ch 1, 2 sc in first st, sc in each st to marker, patt as established to next marker, sc in each st to last st, 2 sc in last st, turn. [43 (43, 47, 47, 47) sts]

7 • Rep step 6 (last 2 rows) 5 (5, 3, 3, 3) more times. [53 (53, 53, 53, 53) sts]

8 • Work 3 rows even in st patt as established.

NEXT ROW (INC): Ch 1, 2 sc in first st, sc in each st to marker, patt as established to next marker, sc in each st to last st, 2 sc in last st, turn. [55 (55, 55, 55, 55) sts]

9 • Rep step 8 (last 4 rows) 12 (12, 14, 14, 14) more times. [79 (79, 83, 83, 83) sts]

10 • Work even in st patt as established until 18 (18½, 19, 19½, 20)" from beg. Remove markers. Fasten off.

Hood

1 • Sew back to front at shoulders.

2 • With RS facing, join A with sc (count as st) at right front neck edge and work evenly spaced sts as foll:

ROW 1 (RS): RIGHT FRONT NECK BASE: 5 sc;
RIGHT FRONT SLOPE: 14 (14, 16, 16, 18) sc;
BACK NECK: 25 (27, 29, 33, 35) sc;
LEFT FRONT SLOPE: 14 (14, 16, 16, 18) sc;
LEFT FRONT NECK BASE: 6 sc, turn. [65 (67, 73, 77, 83) sts]

3 • ROW 2: Ch 1, sc in first st, *hdc in next st, sl st loosely in next st*, rep from * to * to last 2 sts, hdc in next st, sc in last st, turn.

4 • ROW 3: With B, ch 1, sc in first and each st to end, turn.

5 • ROW 4: With C, ch 1, sc in first 32 (33, 36, 38, 41) sts, sc in next st, pm in st just completed, sc in each st to end, turn.

Note: In subsequent rows, move marker to same st in current row as it's encountered.

6 • ROW 5 (INC): With D, ch 1, sc in each st to 1 st before st with marker, 2 sc in next st, sc in next (marked) st, 2 sc in next st, sc in each st to end, turn. [67 (69, 75, 79, 85) sts]

Starting with row 2 of Seeded Stripes st patt, cont in st patt as established and inc as foll:

7 • Work 3 rows even in st patt as established.

NEXT ROW (INC): Patt as established until 1 st before marker st, 2 sc in next st, sc in next (marked) st, 2 sc in next st, patt as established to end, turn. [69 (71, 77, 81, 87) sts]

8 • Rep step 7 (last 4 rows) 6 more times. [81 (83, 89, 93, 99) sts]

9 • Work even in st patt as established until 12" from beg of hood, ending with WS row complete.

10 • NEXT ROW (DEC; RS): Patt as established to 2 sts before marker st, sc2tog, sc in next (marked) st, sc2tog, patt as established to end, turn. [79 (81, 87, 91, 97) sts]

11 • Rep step 10 (last row) 11 more times. [57 (59, 65, 69, 75) sts]
Fasten off.

12 • Fold upper edge of hood in half vertically and WS tog. Sew tog at upper edge.

Front Edging

1 • With RS facing, join A with sc (count as st) at bottom, center front, corner of right front and work evenly spaced sts as foll:

2 • ROW 1 (RS): RIGHT FRONT: 75 (77, 77, 81, 83) sc; HOOD: 103 sc evenly around front edge of hood. LEFT FRONT: 76 (78, 78, 82, 84) sc evenly down edge to bottom corner, turn. [255 (259, 259, 267, 271) sts]

3 • ROW 2: Ch 1, sc in first st, *hdc in next st, sl st loosely in next st*, rep from * to * to last 2 sts, hdc in next st, sc in last st. Fasten off.

Finishing

1 • On front and back, pm at each side 10 (10, 10½, 10½, 10½)" below shoulder seam. Sew sleeves to body between markers. (See "Inserting Sleeves" on page 93.)

2 • Sew back to front at sides and underarms.

3 • Insert zipper in front opening. (See "Inserting a Zipper" on page 93.)

Delicate yet sturdy, a lace-like edging makes this cardigan dressy enough for an uptown look. But upscale doesn't mean difficult, even though it looks like you need to keep track of several stitch patterns as you work across a row. In fact, you work only one at a time. The garment pieces are stitched from side to side, rather than from bottom to top. When ready to assemble, they're pivoted so that one row edge is at the bottom and the other is at the neck or shoulders.

YARN
Galway from Plymouth, color #113

Extra Small	•	7 balls
Small	•	8 balls
Medium	•	8 balls
Large	•	9 balls
Extra Large	•	10 balls

SUPPLIES
H/8 (5 mm) crochet hook
2 stitch markers
5 buttons, ⅜" wide

GAUGE
15 sts and 18 rows to 4" in Slanted Posts st patt

Slanted Posts

Mock Cable

SLANTED POSTS STITCH PATTERN

Multiple of 2 sts + 5 sts (also add 1 ch for base ch)

FOUNDATION ROW (RS): Sc in 2nd ch from hk (count as st) and in each ch to end, turn.

ROW 2: Ch 1, sc in each st to end, turn.

ROW 3: Ch 1, sc in each of first 3 sts, *ch 1, sk next st, sc in next st*, rep from * to * to end, turn.

ROW 4: Ch 1, sc in each st and ch-sp to end, turn.

ROW 5: Ch 1, [insert hk in first st, YO, draw through lp, tr in first sk st in row below, YO, draw through rem 2 lps on hk, do not sk st (sctr2tog made)], sc in next st, *tr in next sk st in row below, sk st behind tr just made, sc in next st*, rep from * to * to last 3 sts, sc in each st to end, turn.

ROWS 6 AND 7: Ch 1, sc in first and each st to end, turn.

Rows 2–7 form Slanted Posts st patt.

MOCK CABLE BAND

Multiple of 2 sts + 1 st (add 1 ch for base ch)

FOUNDATION ROW (RS): Sc in 2nd ch from hk (count as st) and in each ch to end, turn.

ROW 2: Ch 1, sl st loosely in first and each st to end, turn.

ROW 3: Ch 1, sc in first and each st to end, turn.

ROW 4: Ch 1, sc in first st, *hdc in next st, sl st loosely in next st*, rep from * to * to last 2 sts, hdc in next st, sc in last st, turn.

ROW 5: Ch 1, sc in first and each st to end, turn.

ROW 6: Ch 1, sl st loosely in first and each st to end, turn.

ROW 7: Ch 1, sc in first and each st to end, turn.

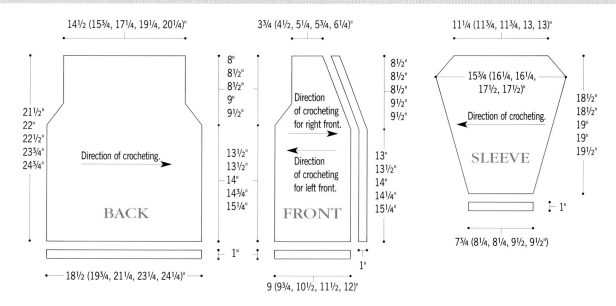

8"
8½"
8½"
9"
9½"

Direction
of crocheting
for right front.

8½"
8½"
8½"
9½"
9½"

15¾ (16¼, 16¼, 17½, 17½)"

Direction of crocheting.

18½"
18½"
19"
19"
19½"

21½"
22"
22½"
23¾"
24¾"

Direction of crocheting.

Direction
of crocheting
for left front.

13½"
13½"
14"
14¾"
15¼"

13"
13½"
14"
14¼"
15¼"

BACK

FRONT

SLEEVE

1"

1"

1"

1"

─ 18½ (19¾, 21¼, 23¼, 24¼)" ─

9 (9¾, 10½, 11½, 12)"

7¾ (8¼, 8¼, 9½, 9½")

SIZING	Extra Small	Small	Medium	Large	Extra Large
To fit bust	31½"	34¼"	37¼"	41"	43¼"
Finished bust	37"	39¾"	42¾"	46¾"	48¾"
Shoulder width	3¾"	4½"	5¼"	5¾"	6¼"
Sleeve length	19½"	19½"	20"	20"	20½"
Center back length	22½"	23"	23½"	24¾"	25¾"

Back

Work sideways from left side to right side.

LEFT ARMHOLE SHAPING

1 • Ch 52 (52, 54, 56, 58).

FOUNDATION ROW (RS): Sc in 2nd ch from hk (count as st) and in each ch to end, turn. [51 (51, 53, 55, 57) sc]

Starting with row 2, work in Slanted Posts st patt (see previous page) and inc as foll:

2 • ROW 2 (INC): Ch 1, 2 sc in first st, sc in next and each st to end, turn. [52 (52, 54, 56, 58) sts]

3 • ROW 3 (INC): Ch 1, sc in each of first 3 sts, *ch 1, sk next st, sc in next st*, rep from * to * to last st, 2 sc in last st, turn. [53 (53, 55, 57, 59) sts]

4 • ROW 4 (INC): Ch 1, 2 sc in first st, sc in each st and ch-sp to end, turn. [54 (54, 56, 58, 60) sts]

5 • ROW 5 (INC): Ch 1, sctr2tog, sc in next st, *tr in next sk st in row below, sk st in previous row behind tr just made, sc in next st*, rep from * to * to last 6 sts, sc in each st to last st, 2 sc in last st, turn. [55 (55, 57, 59, 61) sts]

6 • ROW 6 (INC): Ch 1, 2 sc in first st, sc in each st to end, turn. [56 (56, 58, 60, 62) sts]

7 • ROW 7 (INC): Ch 1, sc in first and each st to last st, 2 sc in last st, turn [57 (57, 59, 61, 63) sts]

Starting with row 2, work in Mock Cable band (see previous page) and inc as foll:

8 • ROW 8 (INC): Ch 1, 2 sc in first st, sl st loosely in each st to end, turn. [58 (58, 60, 62, 64) sts]

9 ROW 9 (INC): Ch 1, sc in first and each st to last st, 2 sc in last st, turn. [59 (59, 61, 63, 65) sts]

BODY

10 • ROW 10 (INC; WS): Ch 23 (25, 25, 27, 29), sc in 2nd ch from hk and each of next 21 (23, 23, 25, 27) ch, sc in next st, *hdc in next st, sl st in next st*, rep from * to * to last 2 sts, hdc in next st, sc in last st, turn. [81 (83, 85, 89, 93) sc]

11 • Work rows 5–7 of Mock Cable band.

12 • Work rows 2–7 of Slanted Posts st patt.

Work rows 2–7 of Mock Cable band.

13 • Rep step 12 (last 12 rows) until 16½ (17¾, 19¼, 21¼, 22¼)" from beg, ending with WS row complete.

Note: Length from beg is width of garment.

RIGHT ARMHOLE SHAPING

Alternating Slanted Posts st patt and Mock Cable band as established, cont as foll:

14 • NEXT ROW (DEC; RS): Patt as established over next 57 (57, 59, 61, 63) sts, sc2tog, turn. Rem sts unworked. [58 (58, 60, 62, 64) sts]

15 • NEXT ROW (DEC): Ch 1, sc2tog, patt as established to end, turn. [57 (57, 59, 61, 63) sts]

NEXT ROW (DEC): Patt as established to last 2 sts, sc2tog, turn. [56 (56, 58, 60, 62) sts]

16 • Rep step 15 (last 2 rows) 2 more times. [52 (52, 54, 56, 58) sts]

17 • NEXT ROW (DEC): Ch 1, sc2tog, patt as established to end, turn. [51 (51, 53, 55, 57) sts]

18 • NEXT ROW: Patt as established to end, turn. Fasten off.

Right Front

Work sideways from right side to center front.

1 • Work as for back, steps 1–13, until 5¾ (6½, 7¼, 7¾, 8¼)" from beg, ending with WS row complete.

RIGHT NECK SHAPING

Alternating Slanted Posts st patt and Mock Cable band as established, cont as foll:

2 • NEXT ROW (DEC; RS): Patt as established across next 76 (78, 80, 84, 88) sts, sc2tog, turn. Rem sts unworked. [77 (79, 81, 85, 89) sts]

3 • NEXT ROW (DEC): Ch 1, sc2tog, patt as established to end, turn. [76 (78, 80, 84, 88) sts]

NEXT ROW (DEC): Patt as established to last 4 sts, sc2tog, turn. Rem sts unworked. [73 (75, 77, 81, 85) sts]

4 • Rep step 3 (last 2 rows) 6 (6, 6, 7, 7) more times. [49 (51, 53, 53, 57) sts]
Fasten off.

Left Front

Work sideways from center front to left side.

LEFT FRONT NECK SHAPING

1 • Ch 50 (52, 54, 54, 58).

FOUNDATION ROW (RS): Sc in 2nd ch from hk (count as st) and in each ch to end, turn. [49 (51, 53, 53, 57) sts]

2 • ROW 2 (INC): Ch 4, sc in 2nd ch from hk (count as st) and in each of next 2 ch, sc in each st to end, turn. [52 (54, 56, 56, 60) sts].

3 • ROW 3 (INC): Ch 1, sc in each of first 3 sts, *ch 1, sk next st, sc in next st*, rep from * to * to last st, 2 sc in last st, turn. [53 (55, 57, 57, 61) sts]

Starting with row 4 of Slanted Posts st patt, cont as foll:

4 • ROW 4 (INC): Ch 4, sc in 2nd ch from hk (count as st) and in each of next 2 ch, patt as established to end, turn. [56 (58, 60, 60, 64) sts]

ROW 5 (INC): Patt as established to last st, 2 sc in last st, turn. [57 (59, 61, 61, 65) sts]

5 • Cont in Slanted Posts st patt and alternating with Mock Cable band, rep step 4 (last 2 rows) 5 (5, 5, 6, 6) more times. [77 (79, 81, 85, 89) sts]

6 • NEXT ROW (INC): Ch 5, sc in 2nd ch from hk (counts as st), sc in each of next 3 ch, patt as established to end, turn. [81 (83, 85, 89, 93) sts]

7 • Work even in alternating Slanted Posts st patt and Mock Cable band as established until 7 (7¾, 8½, 9½, 10)" from beg, ending with WS row complete.

LEFT ARMHOLE SHAPING

8 • Work as for back, steps 14–18 (right armhole shaping). Fasten off.

Sleeve *(Make 2)*

Work from underarm to underarm.

1 • Ch 8 (8, 10, 10, 12).

FOUNDATION ROW (RS): Sc in 2nd ch from hk (count as st) and in each ch to end, turn. [7 (7, 9, 9, 11) sts]

2 • ROW 2 (INC): Ch 6, sc in 2nd ch from hk (count as st) and each of next 4 ch, sc in next and each st to last st, 2 sc in last st, turn. [13 (13, 15, 15, 17) sts]

3 • ROW 3 (INC): Ch 1, 2 sc in first st, pm, sc in each of first 3 sts, *ch 1, sk next st, sc in next st*, rep from * to * to last st, pm, 2 sc in last st, turn. [15 (15, 17, 17, 19) sts]

Alternating Slanted Posts st patt (starting with row 4), with Mock Cable band, cont as foll:

4 • ROW 4 (INC): Ch 6, sc in 2nd ch from hk (count as st), and each of next 4 ch, sc in each st to marker, patt as established to next marker, sc in next st, 2 sc in last st, turn. [21 (21, 23, 23, 25) sts]

5 • ROW 5 (INC): Ch 1, 2 sc in first st, sc in each st to marker, patt as established to next marker, sc in each st to last st, 2 sc in last st, turn. [23 (23, 25, 25, 27) sts] Remove markers.

6 • ROW 6 (INC): Ch 6, sc in 2nd ch from hk (count as st), and each of next 4 ch, patt as established to last st, 2 sc in last st, turn. [29 (29, 31, 31, 33) sts]

7 • ROW 7 (INC): Ch 1, 2 sc in first st, patt as established to last st, 2 sc in last st, turn. [31 (31, 33, 33, 35) sts]

ROW 8 (INC): Ch 6, sc in 2nd ch from hk (count as st), and each of next 4 ch, patt as established to last st, 2 sc in last st, turn. [37 (37, 39, 39, 41) sts]

8 • Rep step 7 (last 2 rows) once more. [45 (45, 47, 47, 49) sts]

9 • NEXT ROW (INC): Patt as established to last st, 2 sc in last st, turn. [46 (46, 48, 48, 50) sts]

NEXT ROW (INC): Ch 6, sc in 2nd ch from hk (count as st) and in each of next 4 ch, patt as established to end, turn. [51 (51, 53, 53, 55) sts]

10 • Rep step 9 (last 2 rows) 3 more times. [69 (69, 71, 71, 73) sts]

11 • Alternating Slanted Posts st patt and Mock Cable band as established, work even until 11¾ (12¼, 12¼, 13½, 13½)" from beg, ending with WS row complete.

12 • NEXT ROW (DEC; RS): Patt as established to last 6 sts, sc2tog, turn. Rem sts unworked. [64 (64, 66, 66, 68) sts]

NEXT ROW (DEC): Ch 1, sc2tog, patt as established to end, turn. [63 (63, 65, 65, 67) sts]

13 • Rep step 12 (last 2 rows) 3 more times. [45 (45, 47, 47, 49) sts]

14 • NEXT ROW (DEC): Ch 1, sc2tog, patt as established to last 6 sts, sc2tog, turn. Rem sts unworked. [39 (39, 41, 41, 43) sts]

NEXT ROW (DEC): Ch 1, sc2tog, patt as established to last 2 sts, sc2tog, turn. [37 (37, 39, 39, 41) sts]

15 • Rep step 14 (last 2 rows) 3 more times. [13 (13, 15, 15, 17) sts]

16 • NEXT ROW (DEC): Ch 1, sc2tog, patt as established to last 6 sts, sc2tog, turn. Rem sts unworked. [7 (7, 9, 9, 11) sts]

17 • Work 1 row even in patt as established. Fasten off.

Back Edging

1 • With RS of back facing, join yarn with sc (count as st) in first row end along bottom edge and work evenly spaced sts in row ends as foll:

ROW 1 (RS): 60 (64, 72, 76, 80) sc to opposite side, turn. [61 (65, 73, 77, 81) sts]

2 • ROW 2: Ch 1, sc in each of first 2 sts, *ch 1, sk next st, sc in each of next 3 sts*, rep from * to * to last 3 st, ch 1, sk next st, sc in each of last 2 sts, turn.

3 • ROW 3: Ch 1, sc in first st, sk next st, *(hdc, ch 1, hdc, ch 1, hdc) in next ch-sp, sk next st, sl st loosely in next st, sk next st*, rep from * to * to last ch-sp, (hdc, ch 1, hdc, ch 1, hdc) in last ch-sp, sk next st, sc in last st. Fasten off.

Right Front Edging

1 • With RS of right front facing, join yarn with sc (count as st) in first row end at bottom edge and work evenly spaced sts in row ends as foll:

Row 1 (RS): 28 (32, 36, 36, 40) sc to opposite side, turn. [29 (33, 37, 37, 41) sts]

2 • Work as for back edging, starting with step 2 (row 2).

Left Front Edging

Work as for right front edging.

Cuff

1 • With RS of sleeve facing, join yarn with sc (count as st) in first row end at bottom edge and work evenly spaced sts as foll:

Row 1 (RS): 36 (36, 36, 40, 40) sc to opposite side, turn. [37 (37, 37, 41, 41) sts]

2 • Work as for back edging, starting with step 2 (row 2).

Front Band

1 • Sew back to front at shoulders.

2 • With RS facing, join yarn with sc (count as st) at lower corner of right front, and work evenly spaced sts in row ends as foll:

Row 1 (RS): Right Front: 41 (41, 43, 45, 47) sc;
Right Front Neck: 25 (25, 25, 28, 28) sc;
Back Neck: 23 (23, 23, 25, 25) sc;
Left Front Neck: 25 (25, 25, 28, 28) sc;
Left Front: 42 (42, 44, 46, 48) sc to bottom corner, turn. [157 (157, 161, 173, 177) sts]

3 • Row 2 (Buttonholes): Ch 1, sc in each of first 117 (117, 118, 129, 130) sts (last 2 sts round corner at top of right front), *ch 2, sk next st, sc in each of next 8 (8, 9, 9, 10) sts*, rep from * to * 3 more times, ch 2, sk next st, sc in last 3 (3, 2, 3, 2) sts, turn.

4 • Row 3: Ch 1, sc in first and each st and ch-sp to end, turn.

5 • Work as for back edging, starting with step 2 (row 2).

Finishing

1 • Sew sleeves into body, centering the top of each sleeve on a shoulder seam. (See "Inserting Sleeves" on page 93.)

2 • Sew back to front at sides and underarms.

Abbreviations and Common Phrases

beg	begin(ning)	**patt(s)**	pattern(s)
blo	back loop only	**pm**	place marker
cb2	2-stitch cable	**R**	right cross (work last post(s) of specified stitch underneath posts just made, see page 84)
cb3	3-stitch cable		
cb4	4-stitch cable		
cb4R	4-stitch cable right cross		
ch(s)	chain(s)	**rem**	remain(s)(ing)
ch-sp	chain-space	**rep**	repeat
cont	continue(ing)	**RS**	right side(s)
cr2	post stitch cross	**rsc**	reverse single crochet
cr2R	post stitch cross right		
cr3	3-stitch post cross	**sc**	single crochet
cr3R	3-stitch post cross right	**sc2tog**	single crochet 2 stitches together (1-stitch decrease)
dc	double crochet	**sctr2tog**	single crochet treble 2 together (1-stitch decrease)
dec	decrease(ing)		
foll	follow(s)(ing)		
FPDC	front post double crochet	**sdc**	spike double crochet
FPDC2tog	front post double crochet 2 stitches together (1-stitch decrease)	**sk**	skip(ped)
		sl st	slip stitch
		sp(s)	space(s)
FPDC3tog	front post double crochet 3 stitches together (2-stitch decrease)	**ssc**	spike single crochet
		st(s)	stitch(es)
		tch	turning chain
FPTR	front post treble crochet	**tog**	together
		tr	treble crochet
FPTR4tog	front post treble crochet 4 stitches together (3-stitch decrease)	**TW2L**	twist 2 posts left
		TW2R	twist 2 posts right
		TWL	twist left
hdc	half double crochet	**TWR**	twist right
hk	hook	**WS**	wrong side(s)
inc	increase(ing)	**YO**	yarn over
lp(s)	loop(s)		

•**Across:** Continue stitching up to—but not including—the stitch noted after "to."

•**As; As for; Work as for:** Stitch the new row or garment piece, following the referenced instructions, up to—but not including—the step, row, or section noted after "to."

•**Current row:** The row in progress.

•**As established:** Maintain the stitch pattern that already exists in previous rows and stitches.

•**First stitch:** The first stitch in the row, closest to the right edge when working from right to left and quite often replaced by a turning chain.

•**In stitch pattern:** Work in the specified combination of rows and stitches as detailed in the referenced pattern.

•**Multiple of:** The number of stitches in a pattern repeat.

•**Move marker:** Remove stitch marker from next stitch in previous row, make new stitch in marked stitch, and place marker in new stitch.

•**Next stitch:** The stitch in the previous or earlier row, immediately beside the one that was just made in the current row.

•**Pattern repeat:** Combination of rows and/or stitches that are continued in sequence.

•**Place marker:** Attach stitch marker between stitches, to specified stitch, or to stitch just worked.

•**Previous row:** The most recently finished row.

•**Row below:** The second row underneath the row in progress.

•**To end:** Continue stitching until row is completed.

•**Turning chain:** One or more chain stitches at the beginning of a row that help "turn" the work and raise the hook to the height of the new row.

•**Two rows below:** The third row below the row in progress.

•**Work even:** Stitch across rows and/or make more rows without decreasing or increasing the number of stitches.

Featured Stitches Guide

Take the first steps toward creating the lush cables and richly textured surfaces of a crocheted Aran sweater. Although the patterns might appear complex, every one that's included in this book is built on a handful of stitches that are explained in this chapter. If Aran crochet is completely new to you, start by learning the front post double crochet stitch on page 88.

Specified stitch + R — *Right Cross Cable*

Crocheters are most familiar with left crossed stitches, which slant to the left. These are the easiest to make because the last post stitch (or stitches) in the group is worked across—and on top of—the previous posts. An example, the post stitch cross (cr2), is shown in figure 2, below. You can see many similar processes in the explanations and figures for the featured stitches on the following pages.

Cables and other crossed stitches can also slant to the right. In these instances, the last post stitch (or stitches) is still worked across the previous posts. For the desired effect, however, the last post(s) must be worked underneath the previous posts—but still on the surface of the crocheted fabric. Compare the right cross version of the post stitch cross, cr2R, (figure 3) to the more familiar left slant (figure 2). Note that when the continuity of a stitch pattern requires a right cross, the specified stitch is followed by an *R*.

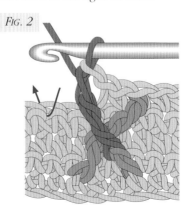

FIG. 2

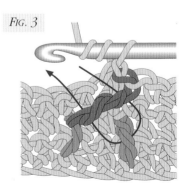

FIG. 3

Bobble *Bobble*

Worked from the wrong side, the finished bobble is a cluster of stitches that looks like a puffball on the right side of the crocheted fabric.

1 Start a double crochet stitch in the usual manner: Wrap the yarn over the hook, insert the hook from front to back in the next stitch, wrap the yarn over the hook, pull the loop to the front of the work, wrap the yarn over

the hook, and pull a loop through the first 2 loops on the hook (figure 4).

Note: The single crochet edge stitch in figures 4, 5, and 6 is not part of the bobble.

2 Start another double crochet stitch: Wrap the yarn over the hook, insert the hook in the same stitch in the previous row from front to back, wrap the yarn over the hook, pull the loop to the

front of the work, wrap the yarn over the hook, and pull the loop through the first 2 loops on the hook (figure 5).

3 Repeat step 2 once more (making one more incomplete double crochet stitch), so that there are 4 loops remaining on the hook.

4 Wrap the yarn over the hook and pull the loop through all the loops on the hook (figure 6).

FIG. 4

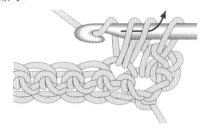

FIG. 5

FIG. 6

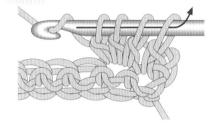

cb2 *Two-Stitch Cable*

This cable is made over 2 adjacent post stitches in the row below.

1 Skip the next front post double crochet stitch in the row below.

2 Work a front post double crochet stitch around the next front post double crochet stitch in the row below (figure 7).

3 Working in front of the front post double crochet stitch just made, make a front post double crochet stitch around the skipped front post double crochet stitch in the row below (figure 8). To complete the row as directed, start the next stitch in the third available stitch in the previous row. Do not work into the 2 stitches behind the 2 front post double crochet stitches just made.

FIG. 7

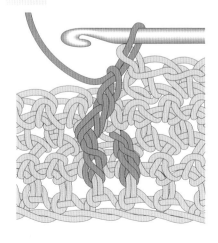

FIG. 8

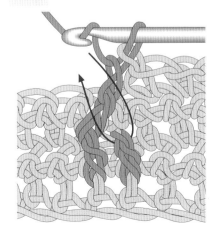

cb3 Three-Stitch Cable

This stitch creates a cable over 3 post stitches in the row below.

1 Skip the first double crochet (or front post double crochet) stitch in the row below.

2 Work a front post double crochet stitch around the post of the second double crochet (or front post double crochet) stitch in the row below.

3 Work another front post double crochet stitch around the post of the third double crochet (or front post double crochet)

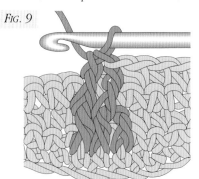

FIG. 9

stitch in the row below (figure 9).

4 Working in front of the 2 stitches just made, work a front post treble crochet stitch around the first (skipped) double crochet (or front post double crochet) stitch in the row below (figure 10). To complete the row as directed, start the next stitch in the fourth available stitch in the previous row. In other words, do not work into the 3 stitches behind the front post double and treble crochet stitches just made.

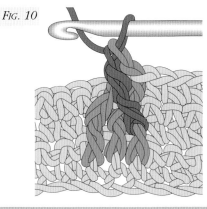

FIG. 10

cb4 Four-Stitch Cable

This cable is made over 4 adjacent post stitches.

1 Skip the first 2 stitches in the row below.

2 Work a front post treble crochet stitch around the post of the third front post double crochet stitch in the row below (figure 11).

3 Work a front post treble crochet stitch around the post of the fourth front post double crochet stitch in the row below (figure 11).

4 Work a front post treble crochet stitch around the first front post double crochet stitch in the row below (figure 12).

5 Work a front post treble crochet stitch around the second front post double

crochet stitch in the row below (figure 13). Do not work into the 4 stitches behind the 4 front post treble crochet stitches just made.

Note: The steps above describe a left cross. To work a right cross (see page 84 for more information), in step 5 work the last 2 front post treble crochet stitches underneath the first 2.

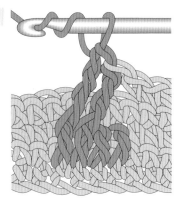

FIG. 11

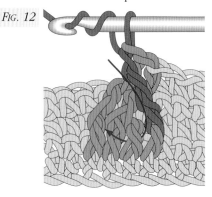

FIG. 12

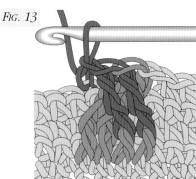

FIG. 13

cr2 Post Stitch Cross

This is built on front post and single crochet stitches.

1 Skip the first front post double crochet stitch in the row below.

2 Work a front post treble crochet stitch around the next (second) front post double crochet in the row below (figure 14.)

3 Skip the stitch in the previous row that's behind the front post treble crochet stitch.

4 Make a single crochet stitch in each of the next 2 stitches (figure 15).

5 Working in front of the front post treble crochet stitch just made, work a front post treble crochet stitch around the first (skipped) front post double crochet stitch in the row below

(figure 16). To complete the post stitch cross, skip the stitch in the previous row (behind the most recent post stitch) and make the next stitch specified.

Note: The steps above describe a left cross. To work a right cross (see page 84 for more information), in step 5 work the last front post treble crochet stitch underneath the first one.

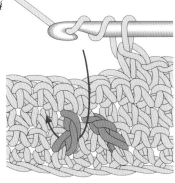
FIG. 14

FIG. 15
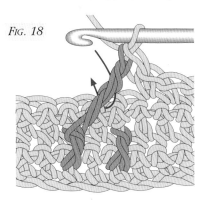

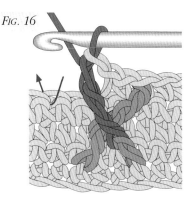
FIG. 16

cr3 Three-Stitch Post Cross

This worked over a post, single crochet, and post stitch in the row below.

1 Skip the first available (unworked) front post double crochet stitch in the row below.

2 Work a front post treble crochet stitch around the second available (unworked) front post double crochet stitch in the row below (figure 17).

3 Skip the next stitch in the previous row, which is behind the front post treble crochet stitch.

4 Make a single crochet in the next stitch (figure 18).

5 Working in front of the front post treble crochet stitch just made, work a front post treble crochet stitch around the first (skipped) front post

double crochet stitch in the row below (figure 19). To complete the 3-stitch post cross, skip the stitch in the previous row (behind the most recent post stitch) and make the next stitch specified.

Note: The steps above describe a left cross. To work a right cross (see page 84 for more information), in step 5 work the last front post treble crochet stitch underneath the first.

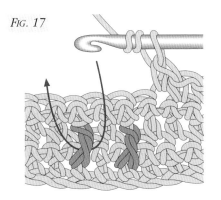
FIG. 17

FIG. 18
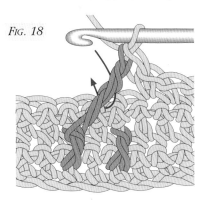

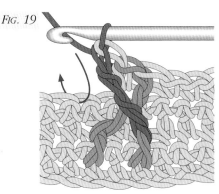
FIG. 19

FPDC and FPTR *Front Post Double and Treble Crochets*

Both the front post double crochet and the front post treble crochet are little more than the basic stitches worked into an earlier row. The illustrations for both of these stitches start with single crochet edge stitches because post stitches shouldn't be worked at an edge.

The post stitch begins by inserting the hook between the first and second stitches (figure 20). Not all experts agree on the placement of the first post. Some start by inserting the hook between the next 2 stitches in the row

below. Both positions are acceptable. It's more important that the placement is consistent.

The following steps, plus figures 20 and 21, explain the front post double crochet. Figure 22 shows a front post treble crochet.

1 Wrap the yarn over the hook. From the front of the work, insert the hook between the current and next stitches in the row below, on the right side of the specified stitch. Now bring the

hook to the front of the work by inserting it, from back to front, on the other side of the next stitch in the row below (figure 20).

2 Wrap the yarn over the hook and then draw a loop to the back, and then to the front of the work.

3 Wrap the yarn over the hook and pull a loop through 2 of the loops on the hook.

4 Rep step 3 once (figure 21).

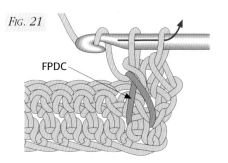

Fig. 20

FPDC

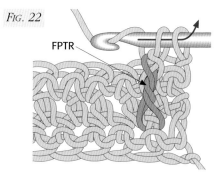

Fig. 22

FPTR

---

rsc *Reverse Single Crochet*

The humble single crochet stitch becomes a delicate corded edging when worked from left to right along the right side of the work.

1 Working in the opposite direction and swinging the hook down and

under your hand, insert the hook, from front to back, in the next stitch to the right (figure 23).

2 Wrap the yarn over the hook and draw a loop through to the front of the work (figure 24).

3 Wrap the yarn over the hook and draw it through both loops on the hook (figure 25).

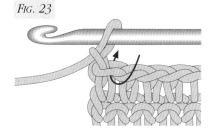

Fig. 23

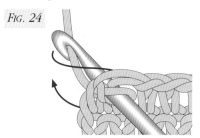

Fig. 24

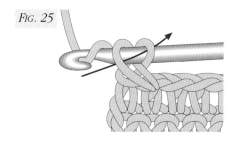

Fig. 25

sdc   *Spike Double Crochet*

Like the more common spike single crochet stitch, this version is also worked by drawing a loop through a lower row.

1 Wrap the yarn over the hook, insert the hook into the next (usually skipped) stitch in the row below, from front to back.

2 Wrap the yarn over the hook, draw a loop through to the front of the work and up to the same height as the current row (figure 26).

3 Complete the double crochet in the usual manner: Wrap the yarn over the hook and pull through the first 2 loops on the hook, wrap the yarn over the hook and pull it through the last 2 loops on the hook.

FIG. 26

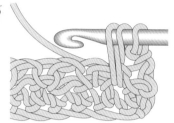

ssc   *Spike Single Crochet*

This is a dramatic stitch that's created by drawing a loop through a lower row and then completing a stitch in the usual manner. Two rows must be completed before starting a row that includes a spike stitch.

1 Insert the hook into the next (usually skipped) stitch in the row below, from front to back (figure 27).

2 Wrap the yarn over the hook, draw a loop through to the front of the work

and up to the same height as the current row (figure 28).

3 Wrap the yarn over the hook and pull it through both loops on the hook (figure 29).

FIG. 27

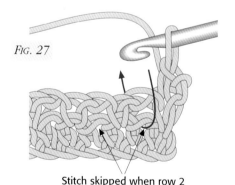

Stitch skipped when row 2
was worked

FIG. 28

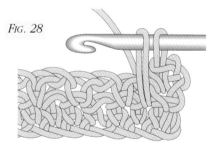

FIG. 29

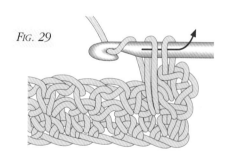

TWL *Twist Left*

The following steps move a post stitch diagonally to the left by 1 stitch position.

1 Make a single crochet stitch in the next stitch (figure 30).

2 In the row below, there's a post stitch that corresponds with the position of the single crochet stitch worked in step 1.

FIG. 30

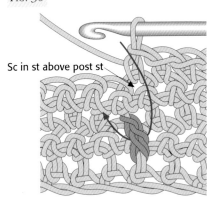

Sc in st above post st

Work a front post double crochet stitch around it (figure 31).

Note: A front post double crochet stitch counts as 1 stitch in the current row. To work even, skip the stitch in the previous row that's behind this post stitch. When a twist left is followed immediately by a twist right, you end up skipping 2 stitches in the previous row (see figure 36 on the next page).

FIG. 31

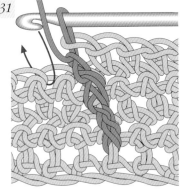

TW2L *Twist Two Posts Left*

Worked over 2 adjacent post stitches in the row below, the TW2L moves 2 post stitches 1 stitch to the left.

1 Make a single crochet stitch in the next stitch.

2 In the row below, there's a post stitch that corresponds with the position of the single crochet stitch worked in step 1. Work a front post double crochet around it (figure 32).

FIG. 32

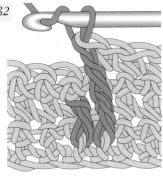

3 Work a FPDC around the next post stitch in the row below that's directly beside the post stitch just worked (figure 33). To complete the row as directed, work the next specified stitch in the third vacant stitch in the previous row. In other words, do not work into the 2 stitches behind the post stitches just made.

FIG. 33

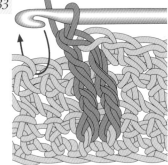

TWR Twist Right

This moves a post stitch diagonally to the right.

1 Make a front post double crochet stitch around the closest post stitch (FPDC or FPTR) in the row below (figure 34).

Fig. 34

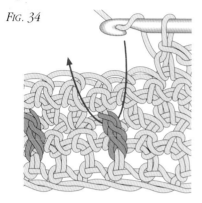

2 Skip the next stitch. Single crochet in the next stitch (figure 35).

Note: A twist right can be worked after a twist left, over 4 stitches. Single crochet stitches are in positions 1 and 4,

Fig. 35

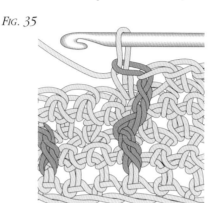

with 2 front post double crochet stitches in the center. The 2 center stitches in the previous row, which are behind the post stitches, are unworked (figure 36).

Fig. 36 **Skip stitches.**

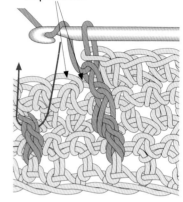

TW2R Twist Two Posts Right

Worked over 2 adjacent post stitches in the row below, the TW2R moves 2 post stitches diagonally to the right by 1 stitch.

1 Make a front post double crochet around the closest post stitch (front post double crochet or front post treble crochet) in the row below (figure 37).

Fig. 37

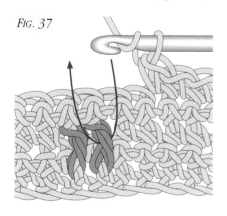

2 Work a front post double crochet around the next post stitch in the row below that is directly beside the post stitch just worked (figure 38).

3 Skip the 2 single crochet stitches behind the 2 front post double crochet

Fig. 38

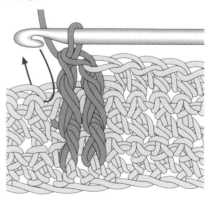

stitches just made, single crochet in next stitch (figure 38).

Note: A TW2L can be followed by a TW2R. In this situation, the 4 center stitches in the previous row, which are behind the post stitches just made, are unworked (figure 39).

Fig. 39

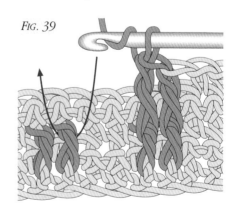

Finishing Techniques

The extra time and care you put into finishing a sweater will give you a professional-looking garment that will wear well for years to come. When your sweater is finished, give it the once-over to make sure the textured stitches are all positioned correctly. Bobbles, for example, may find their way to the wrong side of the fabric, so pull them out and puff them up. If seams or bands aren't quite straight, spot-block them by misting lightly with water and patting them gently in place.

▒ Blocking

The stitch patterns featured in most of the sweaters in this book are heavily textured, so garments must be blocked cautiously. But do block them. At the very least, give them a light treatment to add a bit of polish to the finished sweaters.

Your primary goal when blocking is to coax a garment or its individual pieces to lie flat. If the garment pieces aren't curling, just block the finished, assembled, sweater. As you work, make sure that you don't change the appearance of the stitches or obliterate any of the texture. Also check the yarn label before starting. Natural fibers and fibers with a gentle twist are more sensitive to stretching and pressure than a resilient synthetic fiber. If you're unfamiliar with a yarn, test a swatch first.

Damp blocking is best for crocheted Aran sweaters. Here are the steps.

1 Place a towel on a flat surface and spread the crocheted garment or piece on top. Fasten any buttons or zippers.

2 Pin or shape the selected item to the appropriate measurements, straightening any seams or collar.

3 Place a damp towel on top. Lightly pat the surface to ensure that the moisture works its way into the yarn, but be careful not to crush the pattern or stretch the sweater pieces.

4 With the towel still on top, let the garment dry overnight.

▒ Seaming

The garments in this book were all seamed with a whipstitch. Worked with a firm—not tight—hand, it creates a flat, even seam that holds quite nicely.

1 Thread the yarn on a blunt-tip tapestry needle. For seaming, pick a yarn color that matches one of the edges so that the stitching won't show. If the garment is multicolored, use either the most neutral color or the sweater's main color.

2 With right sides out, pin together the edges of the crocheted pieces that you want to join. Working with the stitch pattern visible, you can avoid errors.

3 Pull the needle and yarn from back to front through the bottom of one of the pieces. Leave a 6" yarn end.

4 Bring the yarn over the matched edges, move up a row or stitch, and again pull the needle through the work from front to back (figure 40). Tug on the yarn until the crocheted edges are beside each other but not overlapped. Continue moving up the length of the edges in this manner (figure 40).

FIG. 40

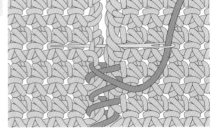

5 It's best to match the rows or stitches of 2 joining edges. A good rule of thumb is to work 1 whipstitch in a single crochet and 2 whipstitches in a double crochet that's at the end of a row. When stitching a drop shoulder sleeve into an armhole, you're attaching stitches to row ends, so the spaces don't match. In this case, take 1 whipstitch in the sleeve and then 1 stitch in the row end of the armhole. Place the stitches evenly so that the seam line doesn't have any gaping holes or lumps.

Inserting Sleeves

Whenever possible, sew sleeves into the armhole after adding the collar and bands for the bottom, front, and neck.

1 Join the back and front at 1 shoulder seam and then stitch the neckband or collar. Stitch the opposite shoulder seam and collar seam.

2 If the body pieces lack armhole shaping, place a stitch marker the specified distance from the shoulder seam on the back and front edges.

3 Fold the sleeve in half lengthwise and place a stitch marker on the top edge at the fold.

4 Spread the joined back and front, right side up, on a table. Place the wider (cap) end of a sleeve, also right side up, between the markers (or bottom of armhole shaping) on one side of the body. Match the shoulder seam to the marker on the sleeve edge (figure 41).

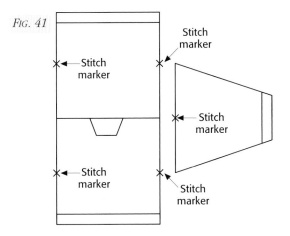

Fig. 41

Stitch marker

Stitch marker

Stitch marker

Stitch marker

Stitch marker

5 Sew the sleeve. After attaching the remaining sleeve in the same manner, refold the body and sleeves to match all loose edges. Join the back to the front by sewing up one side of the body, along the sleeve underarm, and to the end of the cuff. Join the remaining side of the body in the same manner.

Buttonholes

Experts have a great technique for reinforcing buttonholes. When complete, buttons won't fall out of the crocheted holes.

1 Thread a blunt-tip tapestry needle with a length of matching yarn. Secure the yarn end to the wrong side of the work by pulling it through the surface of the stitches for 1", then back again, near an edge of a buttonhole opening.

2 Pull the needle and yarn, from wrong side to right side, through the center opening in the buttonhole.

3 Insert the needle through the crocheted fabric, from the right side to the wrong side, about ¼" away from the edge. Pull the yarn through to the wrong side but don't tighten the stitch.

4 Bring the needle back up through the opening in the center of the buttonhole and through the yarn loop at the edge of the fabric, which was made in step 3. Pull the yarn to tighten the loops without drawing in the fabric edge. Your goal is to create an L-shape at the edge of the buttonhole opening (figure 42).

Fig. 42

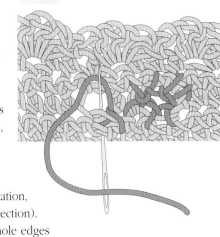

5 Continue making stitches by repeating steps 3 and 4, starting each new stitch (step 3) by moving about ¼" to the left or right (depending on your orientation, but always in the same direction). Work around both buttonhole edges and the corners, if desired.

Inserting a Zipper

1 With the zipper closed, place the right side of the tape against the wrong side of a front opening. Align the bottom of the zipper with the lower edge of the sweater. Let the top of the zipper extend ½" beyond the top of the front neckline, onto the front opening of the hood or collar. Join with quilter's pins.

2 With needle and thread, hand stitch the zipper to the front and beginning of the hood.

3 Place the second front, right side up, on top of the remaining side of the zipper. Pin every few inches.

4 Open the zipper and hand stitch the tape to the front.

Yarn Directory

The color, content, and weight of the yarn you choose will all affect the appearance of the delicate textures and bold interplay of posts and cables in every stitch pattern. Darker colors, for example, cast different shadows than lighter colors. Pure wool creates a denser, less pliable fabric, making it the best choice for a sweater suited to cooler weather and outdoor play. Cotton and smooth, blended yarns with a lighter twist, on the other hand, are appropriate for delicate patterns and more flowing sweaters.

The yarns selected for every garment in *More Crocheted Aran Sweaters* were chosen to enhance the stitch patterns. Use the recommended yarns for the best results. With some experience behind you, you can then experiment by substituting other yarns. The yarns featured in this book are a good place to start. Most of the yarns are interchangeable because they're within the same weight range. But, before starting your sweater, always make a test swatch to check the gauge and behavior of the crocheted fabric.

Brown Sheep Lambs Pride Superwash; 100% wool; 3½ oz/100 g; 200 yds/183 m; featured in Climbing Cables (see page 15)

Brown Sheep Nature Spun Worsted Weight; 100% wool; 3½ oz/100 g; 245 yds/224 m; featured in Country Lane (see page 21)

Butterfly Super 10 (distributed by S. R. Kertzer); 100% mercerized cotton; 4½ oz/125 g; 251 yds/230 m; featured in Double Spiral (see page 47)

Cascade 220; 100% wool; 3½ oz/100 g; 220 yds/201 m; featured in Double Feature (see page 59) and Emerald Isle (see page 33)

Lion Brand Wool-Ease Worsted Weight; 80% acrylic, 20% wool; 3 oz/85 g; 197 yds/180 m; featured in Alpine Meadow (see page 71)

Naturally Yarns Naturelle Aran 10 Ply (distributed by S. R. Kertzer); 100% New Zealand wool; 3½ oz/100 g; 186 yds/170 m; featured in Cables Interrupted (see page 27)

Patons Classic Wool Merino; 100% merino wool; 3½ oz/100 g; 223 yds/204 m; featured in Celtic Garden (see page 65)

Patons Decor; 75% acrylic, 25% wool; 3½ oz/100 g; 210 yds/192 m; featured in Garden Gate (see page 53) and Pastel Heather (see page 43)

Plymouth Encore Worsted Weight; 75% acrylic, 25% wool; 3½ oz/100 g; 200 yds/182 m; featured in Bonnie Highlander (see page 37)

Plymouth Galway; 100% wool; 3½ oz/100 g; 210 yds/192 m; featured in Irish Thistle (see page 77)

Skacel Snow Goose; 100% untreated natural wool; 3½ oz/100 g; 190 yds/174 m; featured in Classic Aran (see page 9)

4

MEDIUM

All of the yarn featured in *More Crocheted Aran Sweaters* are approximately the same weight (thickness), a 4 (medium) on the 1–6 scale developed by the Craft Yarn Council of America.

If you have trouble finding any yarn that's featured in the sweaters in this book, contact the manufacturer for the name of the nearest retailer. Some yarn companies will sell direct to the consumer.

Brown Sheep Company, Inc.
100662 County Road 16
Mitchell, NE 69357
Telephone: (308) 635-2198
Web site: www.brownsheep.com
Email: bsc_co@brownsheep.com

Cascade Yarns, Inc.
PO Box 58168
Tukwila, WA 98138
Telephone: (800) 548-1048
Web site: www.cascadeyarns.com
Email: sales@cascadeyarns.com

Lion Brand Yarn Company
34 West 15th Street
New York, NY 10011
Telephone: (800) 258-YARN
Web site: www.lionbrand.com
Email: customerservice@lionbrandyarn.com

Patons
PO Box 40
Listowel, ON
Canada N4W 3H3
Telephone: (888) 858-4258
Web site: www.patonsyarns.com

Plymouth Yarn Company Inc.
PO Box 28
Bristol, PA 19007
Telephone: (800) 523-8932
Web site: www.plymouthyarn.com
Email: pyc@plymouthyarn.com

S. R. Kertzer Limited
50 Trowers Road
Woodbridge, ON
Canada L4L 7K6
Telephone: (800) 263-2354
Web site: www.kertzer.com
Email: info@kertzer.com

The Skacel Collection, Inc.
PO Box 88110
Seattle, WA 98138
Telephone: (800) 255-1278
Web site: www.skacelknitting.com
Email: info@skacelknitting.com

Acknowledgments

There were so many creative minds involved in bringing this book together, as well as a support network that kept the project going.

I would like to express my deepest appreciation to my editor Susan Huxley. Her constant guidance, patience, and moral support have meant a great deal to me. Working with her was a truly enjoyable experience, and I have learned much from her wisdom.

The wonderful people at Martingale & Company deserve thanks for believing in this book and allowing me to share my designs with my fellow crocheters.

I would also like to thank John Hamel for his stunning fashion photography and Robert Gerheart for the enticing photos of the stitch patterns. I also appreciate Barbara Field's page design and layout, as well as her hard work in seeing this project come to life.

I would especially like to thank my family members for their encouragement, patience, and support. My husband, Todd, has always encouraged me to reach higher for my dreams. My two little sweethearts gave me a little breathing room to accomplish this project. And my mom and my dad have always been there for me, to pick me back up, to dust me off, and say to me, "Try again." I love you guys.

Finally, I'd like to express my gratitude to the many yarn companies who helped make the designs in this book a reality with their generous yarn contributions. Their support and encouragement are greatly appreciated. A special thank-you goes out to Ingrid Skacel at The Skacel Collection, Inc.; Joan Somerville at Cascade Yarns, Inc.; Doris Erb at Patons/Spinrite; Uyvonne Bigham at Plymouth Yarn Company Inc.; Josie Dolan at S. R. Kertzer Limited; Judy Wilson at Brown Sheep Company, Inc.; and the helpful staff at Lion Brand Yarn Company.

Jane Snedden Peever

Meet the Author

Jane Snedden Peever continues her ascent as the premier designer of Aran stitch patterns for crocheted sweaters with this, her second book. Full of more innovative designs, this book continues in the same vein as the first, *Crocheted Aran Sweaters* (Martingale & Company, 2003).

This woman is a rare talent. She has an instinctive understanding of stitch patterns, which allows her to create innovative Aran patternwork for crocheters. Where others may falter with a pattern or reach for pen and paper to work out details, Jane just keeps on stitching.

An inventor at heart, Jane loves to play with new ideas and concepts. She strives for designs that are a balance between trendy and classic, and she loves a challenge. She enjoys trying to prove that all things are really possible with crochet.

Her natural abilities surfaced when she was a youngster. When her mother gave her a scarf to practice stitching, Jane set it aside and started a Nordic sweater. Jane's school years were spent personalizing patterns and, upon graduating, she worked in retail management and as a design apprentice for a few years.

The turning point in her design career was the opening of her yarn shop. With a spectacular selection of yarn at her fingertips, she began creating unique pieces for herself, family, friends, and customers. Soon she was publishing her own patterns.

Now a full-time designer, Jane is a professional member of the Crochet Guild of America. From her rural home she creates sweaters for yarn companies and major publications, and designs sterling silver jewelry for art galleries and boutiques. Jane lives in Pembroke, Ontario, with her husband, Todd, and her two energetic children, Tessa and Thomas.

Jane would love to hear from crocheters. Her email address is tjpeever@nrtco.net.